T0079721

AVOCADO

Edible

Series Editor: Andrew F. Smith

EDIBLE is a revolutionary series of books dedicated to food and drink that explores the rich history of cuisine. Each book reveals the global history and culture of one type of food or beverage.

Already published

Avocado

A Global History

Jeff Miller

REAKTION BOOKS

For Ken Smith: a good friend and ardent supporter.
Your support of others goes neither unnoticed nor unappreciated.

Published by Reaktion Books Ltd
Unit 32, Waterside
44–48 Wharf Road
London N1 7UX, UK
www.reaktionbooks.co.uk

First published 2020

Copyright © Jeff Miller 2020

All rights reserved
No part of this publication may be reproduced, stored in a retrieval
system, or transmitted, in any form or by any means, electronic,
mechanical, photocopying, recording or otherwise, without the prior
permission of the publishers

Printed and bound in India by Replika Press Pvt. Ltd

A catalogue record for this book is available from the British Library

ISBN 978 1 78914 203 7

Contents

I

The History of the Avocado

For a generation who grew up with avocado in the sandwich they bought at Pret A Manger, or who dipped into a giant bowl of guacamole at a Super Bowl party, or stopped at their local coffee shop for an espresso and a slice of avocado toast, the avocado must seem as though it has always been there. Such is its ubiquity today. But as little as one hundred years ago, the avocado was scarcely known outside of its ancestral homeland in the verdant valleys of Michoacán.

Today the avocado is as familiar as the apple, which it may soon displace as the most commonly consumed fruit in the world. The story of how a fruit that isn't sweet, becomes bitter when it is cooked, has an unfamiliar and slippery texture and is a very peculiar shade of green when ripe came to conquer the imagination of the world is an interesting one indeed. It is a story of lucky finds in orchards, a creative and Herculean marketing effort, and a seismic shift in people's attitudes towards nutrition; of a berry that overcame the obstacles of unfamiliarity, high price and a distinctly odd mouthfeel to become the darling of everyone from the fashionistas of Paris to the cattle ranchers of Patagonia. This is the story of the avocado.

In the Beginning

Avocados are in the Laureceae or laurel family. Laureceae are basal angiosperms, which are one of the oldest groups of flowering plants on the planet, dating back over 100 million years. Laurels have been notable plants for millennia, and the terms *laurels* and *laureate* denote excellence. The terms *poet laureate* and *baccalaureate* derive from the name of the laurel tree. The sweet bay, or bay laurel, has the Latin name *Laurus nobilius*, or noble laurel. The laurel family, which is in the order *Ranales*, includes several trees that are culinarily and economically important, including cinnamon, sassafras, cassia, sweet bay, California bay and camphor. Avocados are the most economically important of them all.

Botanically, avocados are in the genus *Persea*, and are probably the most familiar plant in that plant family for the majority of people. The earliest *Persea* evolved on the first supercontinent, Gondwanaland. As the early supercontinents formed and broke up, *Persea* migrated with various smaller landmasses and travelled with what became Africa and Europe as well as North and South America. Examples of *Persea* are still found in various places around the world, but they thrived particularly in the landmasses that became North and South America, prospering in the warm, moist climatic conditions of the subtropics on these continents.

The avocado is a product of the current geologic era, the Cenozoic. When the volcanic eruptions of the late Neogene period created the Mesoamerican land-bridge that joined the continents of North and South America, the habitat that was created proved perfect for the evolution of the tree we now call the avocado. The ecological conditions of this area also gave us the plants that would evolve into corn (maize), chilli peppers, squashes, vanilla and chocolate. While avocados are grown today on every continent except Antarctica, the heritage of the tree is firmly associated with the Americas and the species is known as *Persea americana*.

Given the intense selection for fruit quality by humans over many millennia, the avocado is usually considered a domesticated plant, but the argument could be made that the avocado is only a semi-domesticate, owing to its heterozygous nature. An organism is considered heterozygous when genes for different characteristics are located at the same place within a chromosome. Which gene is expressed when the organism reproduces is random, so, as in humans, offspring are related to the parent, but are never exact copies of one parent or the other. The avocado is considered highly heterozygous by botanists and breeders because seeds grown from trees are extremely unpredictable when it comes to the resulting fruit quality. As is the case with apple seeds, trees grown from the seeds of a particular avocado tree are unlikely to resemble the parent tree. To get a scion that is a replica of the parent, it must be propagated vegetatively through budding and grafting. For orcharding purposes, avocado trees are almost universally propagated through grafting and budding, though researchers grow many trees from seed because desirable characteristics may be manifested in these offspring that were not present in the parent tree.

Avocados are often referred to as cultigens, which means they are a domesticated species that has been so altered from its original ancestors that it is considered a distinct and unique species. Most of the plants that we use for food today are cultigens, including corn, broccoli and sugar cane.

The Three Races of Avocado

The avocado, or *Persea americana*, is a subspecies of the genus *Persea*. *Persea americana* has been further subclassified into three landraces: the Mexican, the Guatemalan and the West Indian. Genetic analysis of avocados suggests that two of these races, the Mexican and the Guatemalan, are probably the result of the dispersal of the seed from the earliest forms of the plant by megafauna into regions that favoured unique species development based on regional ecological conditions. The third race, the West Indian, is probably a product of early attempts at domestication by early Mesoamericans. There are still many undomesticated species of avocados in the original ranges of the three races. The fruits of these undomesticated plants tend to be small and round and have a fairly high seed-to-flesh ratio. These non-domesticates are often referred to generically as *criollo*. *Criollos* tend to be the size of goose or

Avocados (*Persea americana*), Kampala, Uganda.

Criollo-type avocados.

turkey eggs and have a dark, blue-blackish skin even before they ripen. These types were likely the ones eaten and spread by the megafauna.

The Mexican race of avocados is known in Spanish as *aoacatl*. This race developed in the cool tropical and subtropical highlands of central Mexico. They do best in altitudes above 2,400 metres (7,870 ft) in areas that have lower levels of humidity and rainfall than the surrounding lowlands. The combination of the geography of this area and the weather patterns in the late Pleistocene aided the development of the avocado as a desirable fruit. The Mexican race, as far as current evidence allows us to draw conclusions, was the first to be used by humans for food and was even in use in Mesoamerica prior to the development of purposeful agricultural and horticultural practices by the indigenous populations.

The Guatemalan race of avocados are known in Spanish as *quilaoacatl*. This is a tropical highland race that thrives in warmer and moister climates than the Mexican race. It grows best at altitudes between 800 and 2,400 metres (2625 ft and 1.5 mi.).

The West Indian race of avocados are known in Spanish as *tlacacolaocatl*. Also referred to as the Antillean race, this race grows in warm, moist tropical and subtropical areas between sea level and 800 metres. They are really at their best in elevations below 400 metres (1,310 ft) but will grow relatively well to the upper limits of their range. This race is the best performer of the three in saline soils, so we may see more of them in international commerce as soil salination becomes a critical issue in the wake of orchard irrigation in most of the places where commercial avocado cultivars are grown today.

The separate grouping of the West Indian race may be flawed nomenclature. Louis O. Williams and other botanists argue for there being only two races of avocado, the Mexican and the Guatemalan. Based on genetic markers, they argue that the West Indian race is a subordinate of the Mexican race. There is little evidence of the West Indian race being in place much before the arrival of the Spanish in the fifteenth century. Mesoamerican peoples probably brought the seeds of Mexican race avocados to the northern coastal regions of South America and the Antilles, or West Indies. There is evidence of an extensive canoe-based trading network between the mainland and islands of South America and Central America prior to the arrival of Europeans. The West Indian race is probably the result of human selection of plants that were grown from seed and brought from the Central American mainland, with the ones that were able to prosper in the new climate being selected and replanted based on the ability to grow well and produce desirable fruit.

A good specimen of the West Indian race of avocado, grown at Tapachula, Chiapas, Mexico. The fruit weighs nearly 900 g (2 lb).

The avocado probably only beat the Spanish to the Antilles and the Inca empire by a nose, historically speaking. But without the needed historical and horticultural background, the Spaniards assumed that West Indian race cultivars were native to the areas where they were first seen. The name West Indian was given to the race because of descriptions provided by explorers and conquerors after they encountered it on the islands.

The Spanish themselves were responsible for the initial global spread of the avocado. They observed that the fruit grew freely, was nutritious and didn't compete for space with cash-generating crops like sugar cane. Avocados were frequently used as food for enslaved people working the sugar plantations in the Caribbean, and as the Spanish colonial plantation model spread to places like the Philippines, slave-holders brought them along to feed the workers.

Avocados and Megafauna

Avocados co-evolved with the megafauna of the late Pleis-tocene epoch. The earliest versions of the avocado, the ones that resemble today's *criollos*, were eaten by the herbivorous megafauna of Mesoamerica. The avocado was dependent on herbivores such as the giant ground sloth, the toxodon (hippo-like, but terrestrial), gomphotheres (a four-tusked distant relative of the elephant), giant camels and giant armadillos to distribute their seeds. All of these animals were large. One author says the giant ground sloth was as big as a modern delivery lorry and up to 5.5 metres (18 ft) tall, dwarfing a modern African elephant. Even the smallest of them was

Charles R. Knight, *Gomphotherium angustidens*, 1901, gouache on paper.

Pavel Riha, *Giant Armadillo (Glyptodon)*, digital rendering.

bigger than a modern passenger car. Herbivores of that size would have required a prodigious amount of food just to survive; much smaller modern-day elephants require 90–180 kilograms (200–400 lb) of food a day.

Given the relatively low calorie-to-mass ratio of leaves, grasses, sedges and other leafy vegetation, most herbivorous animals seek out other types of flora to avail themselves of the caloric boost they provide. Good supplemental choices include fruits, nuts and tubers. Most animals are attracted to fruit because of the energy contained in its sugars. The most successful fruits likely evolved with higher sugar levels than their competitors as a strategy to ensure that they would be eaten and their seeds would be spread via the excretions of the eater.

Plants with small fruits and seeds tend to be more plentiful at the forest's edge or in ecotones, the border areas between ecological biomes. Plants with large seeds, like the avocado, tend to be concentrated in the interior of a forest. To get animals to venture into the interior, find them and eat them, and hence spread their seeds, they tend to be richer in nutrition than fruits with smaller seeds. Describing his travels to find new avocado varieties, Wilson Popenoe, the famous botanist and scientific explorer, reported that he found the smallest avocado varieties at the forest edge and larger specimens deeper in the interior.

Darwin proposed that the juicy flesh and sugary energy of fruits was 'a toll' collected by the animals in exchange for the dispersal and survival of the fruit. In the case of the avocado the toll would have been high-quality energy calories and a valuable source of vegetable fat. Early humans were probably attracted to the fruit for the same reasons as the megafauna. The ethnobotanist Gary Nabhan argued in 1987 at the 10th Annual Meeting of the Society of Ethnobiology that 'megafaunal selection of fruit qualities preadapted them to human use in ways that made unnecessary much counter-selection by (early) neotropical cultures'. He thinks the megafauna would have selected fruit in much the same way as later humans would have – that is, for flavour, calories and satiety – and that further selection of phenotypes by later-arriving humans would have been more or less unneeded.

The avocado must have evolved to attract the now-extinct megafauna of the Americas to act as their seed dispersers, as the seed is far too large for any modern-day wild mammalian or reptilian fruit-dispersing animal to digest and spread. While jaguars have been observed to eat and successfully pass an avocado seed, they are primarily carnivores, and their con-sumption of the fruit is far too low to serve as an effective evolutionary mechanism. The herbivorous megafauna had throats and digestive tracts that were so large they could swallow avocado fruit whole, which meant there was little or no damage to the seed as it worked its way through the animal. The seeds of the avocado are mildly toxic and have a slight laxative effect. They were probably passed relatively quickly in a well-preserved state. The stone was defecated along with a handy pile of excrement serving as a convenient source of fertilizer for the avocado sapling. We see the same large fauna behaviour in Africa today. Elephants are known to 'raid' avocado plantations in sub-Saharan Africa where they consume avocados and defecate the whole stones. In Mesoamerica, reintroduced megafauna, in the form of horses and cows, will eat ripe avocados and defecate the stones as they move about the countryside. These acts are historical re-creations of the patterns of their megafaunal ancestors.

Plants are quite crafty in getting animals to help them spread their range, and avocados developed a unique strategy in this regard. In botany, the term 'endozoochory' is used to describe the process by which animals eat the seed of a plant, then excrete it undamaged so the seed can grow where it has been deposited. This technique has the benefit of keeping the species alive, but new offspring do not compete with the parent plant for light and nutrients as it would if the seed grew alongside the parent. In the case of the avocado, the endocarp (the innermost layer of the fruit, surrounding

Avocado crate art for Black Gem.

the seed) is slippery and aids the exit of the seed from the digestive tract of the animal that consumes it. It is also bitter and mildly toxic, which discourages the animal from chewing on the stone, which would cause it not to be viable upon deposition. Even the smell of the avocado evolved to attract dispersers. The aroma of the avocado is determined by terpenes, aromatic essential oils, in its fruit and flowers, a trait it shares with the cannabis plant. The terpenes in avocados signalled the presence of medium-chain fatty acids, essential nutrients for the megafauna.

The author Connie Barlow argues in her book *The Ghosts of Evolution* that the avocado is 'overbuilt'. She says it evolved to pass through the digestive tracts of beasts like the gomphotheres intact, a feature that it does not require today. She writes, 'An avocado sitting in a bin at the grocery store is thus biology in a time warp. It is suited for a world that no longer exists. The fruit of the avocado is an ecological anachronism. Its missing partners are the ghosts of evolution.'

The range of these mega-herbivores was quite extensive, and the ancestors of the modern avocado used their animal dispersal agents to spread from their original home in the subtropical highlands of central Mexico down through what are today the countries of Central America and even into the northernmost reaches of South America. The climate in the areas that the avocado spread into were hospitable enough for the seeds to take root and grow, but different enough for speciation of *Persea* to begin. The result was the beginning of the major avocado phenotypes, or races.

After the extinction of the American megafauna at the end of the Pleistocene, the fruit would have dropped to the ground directly under the tree with no other way to spread itself, a poor evolutionary strategy and one that would not account for the range of the early avocado. The Pleistocene extinction affected about 70 per cent of the megafauna in North America and nearly 80 per cent of the megafauna in South America. The only remaining herbivores large enough to eat the fruit and disperse the seed through defecation were horses, bison and elephants, none of which were present in the places where the avocado grew.

The avocado evolved to fit the needs of its megaherbivore dispersers. As Barlow writes, 'After 13,000 years, the avocado is clueless that the great mammals are gone.' After the death of its primary dispersers, the avocado had to bide its time waiting for a new disperser to come along and continue its spread. After the Pleistocene, all the avocado's megafaunal dispersers had disappeared, but it had longevity on its side to help it survive until a new dispersing animal came along to help it out. An avocado tree can live for as long as five hundred years in the wild. A Hass avocado tree in Southern California is still bearing fruit robustly at nearly one hundred years old, and wild trees estimated to be nearly four hundred years old are bearing fruit in the subtropical highlands of Central Mexico. As Barlow continues, for a species that developed millions of years ago, 'the passage of 13,000 years [since the Pleistocene extinction] is too soon to exhaust the patience of the genus *Persea*.'

The age of the megafauna came to an end as humans, who crossed from Asia into the Americas using the land-bridge at the Bering Strait, began to spread across the Americas. Whether they were hunted to death for their meat, or whether they could no longer compete with humans for food, the extinction of the giant herbivores should have signalled the end of the line for fruits like the avocado. But the avocado did survive, an example of what the paleobotanists D. H. Janzen and P. S. Marten called, in 1982, 'neotropical anachronisms'.

Without large mammals like the giant ground sloth to carry the seed away from the parent, the avocado seed would most often have rotted where it fell, and those that did grow would have had to compete with the parent tree for light and food, not an ideal strategy for reproduction and survival. Today the dispersers of avocado seeds are human, and we will shape the forward evolution of the avocado just as surely as the toxodon did in the Pleistocene.

Early Mesoamericans

Without another dispersal animal, the avocado would likely have done a slow fade-out from the horticultural panorama of the world. It probably would have lost its place in the small ecological niche of the central Mexican highlands to something more fecund, transportable, sweeter or tastier. But happily, for us and for the avocado, the perfect avocado stone dispersal animal was working its way down the North American continent from the exposed land-bridge from Asia: the rapidly spreading *Homo sapiens*.

Anatomically modern humans began their great migration out of Africa between 70,000 and 100,000 years ago. By about 20,000 years ago they had spread across all the continents reachable by foot and had even managed to work their way across the archipelago of Indonesia to settle in Australia. Around that 20,000-year-ago mark, an event called the Last Glacial Maximum caused a dramatic drop in sea levels and exposed what we now call the Bering Land Bridge. Humans were able to cross into the Americas from Asia and begin their spread southward. After 6,000 years or so, they had arrived and settled the subtropical highlands of central Mexico. Archaeological remains suggest that they began to exploit the fruit of the avocado tree early in the development of organized cultural groups in the region. When early users of the fruit took the avocados back to their encampments and discarded the bitter stones, the new human dispersers of the fruit made sure the fruit survived and increased its range. We have evidence of human–avocado interaction dating back at least 9,000 years. The arid Coxcatlan caves in the Mexican state of Puebla contain the remains of avocados that could easily have been brought up from the humid canyons in the area. It is certainly logical to think that early Mesoamericans would have been attracted to avocados, given the high levels of fat, calories and protein in the fruit.

The Mokaya are considered the earliest organized social group in Mesoamerica and are thought to have been the first group to begin domesticating cacao and maize. While the name Mokaya means 'the corn people' in the Mixo-Zoquean language they were thought to speak, evidence suggests that native fruits like the avocado were more important to their diet than the small early versions of maize. The earliest organized groups like the Mokaya probably represented the forefront of a transition from wandering explorer-settlers to an organized hunter-gatherer culture. While the transition to a settled horti-culturalist-pastoralist society was still in the future for these Mesoamerican groups, we suspect the Mokaya and others managed natural stands of avocado as a food source. There isn't evidence of active efforts to domesticate the avocado by the Mokaya, but as predecessors of the Olmec and Mayan cultures who did actively manage avocado orchards, they must have had significant knowledge of avocado management.

The Norte Chico or Caral-Supa civilization, the earliest organized cultural group in northern South America, used avocados as a food source as well. This group was probably more dependent on sweet potatoes, squashes and beans for their primary nutrition, but excavated sites show a level of avocado consumption that is greater than that of maize. The importance of the avocado to the Norte-Chico is supported by the fact that avocado plant remains have been found in ceremonial mounds in Huaca Prieta, north of what is now Lima, Peru. Sir James Frazer, in his classic *The Golden Bough*, writes of a festival held by the Indians of northern Peru to make 'alligator pears' ripen and become more flavourful:

> The festival lasted five days and five nights, and was preceded by a fast of five days during which they ate neither salt nor pepper and refrained from their wives. At the festival men and boys assembled stark naked in an open space among the orchards, and ran from there to a distant hill. Any woman they overtook along the way was violated.

By the time this area was conquered by the Inca in the century or so before the arrival of the Spaniards, avocados were growing in managed orchards.

Olmecs, Mayans and Aztecs were among the first highly organized social groups in Mesoamerica. They all valued the avocado highly enough as a food source that representations of them and glyphs meaning 'avocado' occur with high frequency in their stonework. In excavated Olmec sites, avocados tend to be the most abundant food remains. In these cultures, the avocado was often referred to as a 'gift of the gods'. Given the ease with which they grew, their nutritive value and their delicious flavour, it is easy to see why the avocado was a favourite food source of these early Mesoamerican and South American cultures.

These groups increased the range of the avocado as they distributed it along their extensive trade routes in North,

Central and South America. Useful plants such as cacao, vanilla, avocado, squash, beans, peppers and maize were spread along these trade routes. One side effect of this constant movement and farming would have been early hybrids of the plants. Certainly, the germplasm from the primary races of avocado would have intermingled and, given avocados' heterozygous nature, useful fruits would have appeared. Archaeological evidence shows fruit size increasing throughout the pre-Columbian era, suggesting that selection for fruit size was ongoing. People who planted avocado trees and relied on them for food security would undoubtedly select for desirable characteristics as they made planting decisions.

Avocados were a key food source that allowed the growth and spread of these groups. Some of the places where avocados were cultivated most intensively by these groups had higher population densities than they do today, speaking to the importance of the nutrition provided by the avocado fruit. In many excavations of their cultural sites, avocados represent the largest amount of biological residue, further buttressing this argument.

The avocado was extremely important to the Maya. The Mayan holy book, the Popul Vah, mentions the avocado in conjunction with the great creation story. In this story, humans were created from *masa* made with white and yellow maize, and fruit trees were provided for their sustenance. For the Maya and other groups in Mesoamerica, arboriculture was an important component in their survival strategy. It was probably the Maya who began the domestication of the avocado as they began to select trees for desirable culinary traits and plant them as part of their arboreal ecosystem.

Tomb carvings in the great Mayan city of Palenque show avocado trees. One of the greatest Mayan rulers, King Pakal the Great, was buried in Palenque, and his tomb has ten different trees carved upon it, one of which is the avocado. Pakal's grandmother, the Lady Kanal-Ika, is shown emerging from the carving of the avocado tree on his sarcophagus. The Maya usually cultivated trees around their homes as they felt their ancestors would be reborn as trees, and sometimes they would plant avocado trees on the graves of the newly buried.

In the town of Pusilha, Belize, are the remains of an early Mayan city. The municipal symbol of the town is the avocado, in much the same way that the pomegranate is the municipal symbol of modern Granada, Spain. The glyph for the avocado can be found in many stone carvings in the excavated ruins. The rulers of the city were known as 'the Lords of the Avocado'.

The Mayan calendar, known today as the Haab Calendar, is based on seasonal agricultural products. The fourteenth 'month' of the calendar is the month of the avocado. The glyph for this month is called Uniw or Uniiw. (Some sources think the month was called K'ank'in.) This glyph is a common carving in Mayan stonework, attesting to the importance of the fruit in the culture.

The avocado was of considerable importance to the Aztecs, who made their capital in México-Tenochtitlán, or what we now call Mexico City. The name of the important Aztec city of Ahuacatlan means 'where the avocado abounds'. Its glyph is an avocado tree with teeth. Early tribal clients of the Aztec often gave fruit as tribute to their overlords in the capital city of Tenochtitlán, and avocados were among the most desirable of these. The avocado was a favourite of the Aztec nobility. In their belief system, the avocado fruit gave strength. In this culture, like many early cultures, an animal, vegetable or fruit was thought to have transferable qualities based on its physical appearance. The small *criollo*

Deborah Griscom Passmore, early 'Mexican' no. 36 variety, *criollo* style, 1906.

avocados of the period were thought to resemble a vigorous testicle and therefore, by eating them, your testicles could be vigorous too. The aroma of the ripening avocado was thought to be a powerful aphrodisiac, and legend has it that women from noble Aztec families were not allowed outside during the harvest period for fear the aroma would drive them wild with desire and make them unchaste.

The Inca were eating avocados at the time of the initial Spanish contact, but like the peoples of the Antilles, they got the fruit just ahead of the arrival of the Spanish. The Inca got the avocado when they conquered the Caral-Supa civilization in what is now north-central Ecuador. The monarch Tupac Inca Yupanqui conquered an area known as Palta and brought the fruit back to the warm valleys near his capital of Cuzco. The fruit was called *palta* after the place it was brought from. It is still referred to as *palta* in modern Peru and Ecuador.

Spanish Contact and the Colonial Period

From the earliest time of European contact with the New World, explorers wrote about the avocado. The first mention of an avocado by a European was in the travelogue *Suma de geographia que trata de todas las partidas y provincias del mundo* by Martín Fernández de Enciso in 1519. De Enciso described the fruit as 'one which looks like an orange and when it is ready for eating it turns yellowish; that which it contains is like butter and is of marvellous flavour, so good and pleasing to the palate that it is a marvellous thing.'

A detailed description followed in 1526 when Fernández de Oviedo wrote:

On the mainland are certain trees called pear trees, but they are not like those of Spain, though held in no less esteem; rather is their fruit of such a nature that they have many advantages over our pears. They are large trees, with broad leaves similar to those of the laurel, but larger and greener. They bear pears weighing a pound and even more, though some weigh less, and the colour and shape is that of true pears, and the rind is somewhat thicker, but softer, and in the centre of the fruit is a seed like a peeled chestnut . . . and between this and the rind is the part which is eaten, which is abundant, and is a paste very similar to butter and very good eating and of good taste.

The fruit Oviedo describes is one that must have been bred for size and flavour by the indigenous people of the area, as wild avocados tend to be much smaller and egg-shaped with a thin edible mesocarp.

In 1554 Francisco Cervantes Salazar noted that avocados were widely available in the markets of Tenochtitlán, the Aztec capital. Writers of this period also commented on the variety of avocado types. Friar Toribio de Benavente wrote, 'The early ones common in all this land and all the year are like early figs. Other avocados are big as large pears and are so good like the best fruit in New Spain. There are others as big as a small pumpkin; ones with a big seed and little flesh and others with more flesh.' Writers who accompanied the earliest explorers and conquerors noted the presence of avocados from central Mexico to northern Peru and in numerous places across the Caribbean.

Early descriptions by the Spanish used terms that would be familiar to people back in Europe. The avocado is described variously as like a fig, like a pear but better, a big tree with

Vicente Albán, *Indian Woman in Special Attire*, c. 1783, oil on canvas.

fruits like courgettes, and like an oak tree with orange leaves and fruits like figs. The early Spanish explorers delighted in the flavours of the fruits of the New World but, like any expatriates, missed the familiar foods from home. One fruit the Spanish missed was the olive. To replace this favourite edible, they would cut up immature avocados and brine them.

Avocado pulp was used by the Spanish to fatten animals for human consumption, especially the pigs they brought with them. Père Labat, a travelling French priest, observed pigs eating avocados that had fallen from trees. He wrote, 'These animals become in consequence marvellously plump, and their flesh contracts an excellent flavour.' One cannot help but contrast this with the feeding of acorns to Iberian pigs to fatten them up, giving the region's renowned jamón ibérico its unique taste.

The earliest accounts written by the Europeans use both the terms *aguacate* and *palta*. In the seventeenth century Fra

Bernabé Cobo wrote, in his *Historia del nuevo mundo* (History of the Inca Empire), 'The palta has a thick skin, more tender and flexible than a Ceuta lemon, green externally, and when the fruit is quite ripe, peeling readily. It has the largest seed that I have ever seen in any fruit, either in the Indies or in Europe.' He goes on to say, '[The flesh] is of whitish green colour, tender, buttery, and very soft. Some people eat it with sugar and salt, others just as it comes from the tree, it being of such a good flavour that it requires no seasoning.'

The first mention of avocados in the English language is from a merchant named Hawkes who toured the Caribbean and wrote an account of his travels in 1589. He used the term *alvacata* when describing the fruit. The English wrested the island of Jamaica from Spanish control in 1655, and a subsequent survey of this new possession two years later shows that by then the avocado was firmly established and widely grown. In 1657 a London publication reporting on the new

José Agustín Arrieta, *Still-life*, *c.* 1870, oil on canvas.

Jamaica colony informed readers that unusual fruits known as *avacatas* were sold in the local markets. It goes on to describe them as 'a pleasant fruit; in season in August, and sold for eight pence per piece'.

In 1672 a physician accompanying the English fleet in the West Indies, William Hughes, visited the island and wrote the first detailed description of the avocado in English. In his book *The American Physician; or, A Treatise of the Roots, Plants, Trees, Shrubs, Fruit, Herbs &c. Growing in the English Plantations in America*, he wrote:

> This is a reasonable high and well spread tree, whose leaves are smooth, and of a pale green colour; the Fruit is of the fashion of a Fig, but very smooth on the outside, and as big in bulk as a Slipper-Pear; of a brown colour, having a stone in the middle as big as an Apricock, but round hard, and smooth; the outer paring or rinde is, as it were, a kind of shell, almost like an Acorn-shell, but not altogether so tough; yet the middle substance (I mean between the stone and the paring, or outer crusty rinde) is very soft and tender, almost as soft as the pulp of a Pippin not over-roasted.

Hughes goes on to say that everyone in Jamaica called it the Spanish pear or shell-pear. He thought it was called a shell-pear because of the hard and crusty skin and to distinguish it from the European, or sweet, pear, which has a soft, edible skin. Hughes thought it was 'one of the most rare and pleasant Fruits of that Island; it nourisheth and strengtheneth the body, corroborating the vital spirits'. He noted that the Spanish were eating an early form of guacamole, with 'the Pulp being taken out and macerated in some convenient thing, and eaten with a little Vinegar and Pepper . . . it is a very delicious meal'. In an early bit of ethnocentrism, he speculated that the Spanish loved them so much because they were useful in 'procuring lust exceedingly'. Another early English mention of the avocado came in 1751 when the future American president George Washington, travelling in the West Indies, reported home in a letter that 'avogago pears' were very popular in Barbados. The first report of an avocado tree being grown in the Old World comes from Valencia, Spain, in 1601.

The avocado found its way around the world quickly in the colonial period, especially to Spanish possessions. A food that was energy-rich and easy to grow would have been attractive to colonial overlords looking for cheap, non-meat foods to feed the populations of their colonies. Avocado trees could be grown on the fringes of sugar plantations to feed the enslaved people working the cane fields, without competing for real estate with the highly profitable sugar cane crop. Even before the arrival of the Europeans, the avocado had spread down the Pacific coast of Middle and South America as well as along the Amazon and several of its tributaries, out to the coastal areas of the Guianas and Venezuela, and beyond to the Antilles. It had reached as far afield as the Philippines by the end of the 1500s and Asia and Africa by the end of the 1700s, and was well established in Hawaii, Australia and the Canary Islands by the beginning of the 1800s. It gained a beachhead in the Mediterranean basin outside Spain in the early 1900s, having been transplanted to Morocco and Palestine.

The Avocado Comes to the USA

Avocados were first brought to the continental United States in 1833 by Henry Perrine, a doctor who served as the u.s. consul in Campeche, Mexico, and was an avid amateur horticulturist. He believed that many of the tropical plants he saw in southern Mexico had commercial potential in his adopted home state, Florida. The avocados he brought back were likely of the Mexican or Guatemalan races or possibly hybrids of the two. The trees did well when they were planted at Perrine's home on the south Florida island Indian Key, but Perrine was later killed in a Native American raid on the island and the plants were not taken up by anyone else for quite some time. Avocados were not cultivated in Florida again until the early 1900s, when seedlings were brought from Cuba and planted around the southern part of the state, with varying levels of success. The locals called them alligator pears, a name still used in the vernacular, but detested by avocado marketers.

While Perrine's trees did not survive, his method of propagation did, and this is his biggest contribution to the American avocado industry. Perrine developed the grafting or budding technique for avocados, the primary method of propagation used today. The process was fast and dependable, and the trees that resulted from grafting bore fruit sooner than those grown from seed. Instead of the genetic roulette that results from trees grown from seed, every tree was true to type. Today, aside from seedlings grown for research purposes, virtually every avocado tree grown in the world comes from budding a desired cultivar onto regionally desirable rootstock.

Two of the cultivars introduced by Perrine, the Trapp and the Pollock, are still widely grown in lowland humid tropical

A sprouting avocado.

regions. The Trapp was not suited to growing in California, the future home of America's largest avocado industry, but it was held in such esteem that the agricultural scientist Wilson Popenoe recalled in his memoir, 'We wanted a California Trapp, an avocado of good commercial characteristics which could be grown from San Diego to Santa Barbara.'

Until the California industry was established, most of the avocados consumed in America came from Florida and were marketed in the big produce hubs of the eastern United States such as New York, Philadelphia and Baltimore. Today Florida produces far fewer avocados than California, but the fruit grown there is still sent to eastern hubs, and consumers in those markets are more likely to find a wider variety of types than shoppers in the rest of the United States, who arely see avocados other than the Hass. Florida produces about 20 per cent of the avocados grown in the United States today, but their market share is shrinking as the best land for growing them is gobbled up by property developers. Still, the contribution made by the early Florida growers is foundational to the modern global avocado industry.

One would think that the Spanish would have brought a plant as valuable as the avocado northwards with them as they migrated north out of Mexico and settled what is now Southern California. But there is no evidence of this. Franciscan monks began establishing missions in what was then called Alta California in 1769 and continued to establish and staff mission churches until the middle of the nineteenth century. Some have suggested that since Hispanic folklore speaks of avocados as aphrodisiacs, the good monks did not want them in their horticultural mix. Whatever the reason, avocados would not be seen in California until more than a hundred years later.

The Avocado Comes to California

The earliest recorded introduction of the avocado into California was on the farm of Dr Thomas White near San Gabriel in 1856. White was a member of the California State Agricultural Society, a private group that had formed in 1854 and served as the de facto State Board of Agriculture until 1919, when California created a State Department of Food and Agriculture. White's seedlings came from Nicaragua and were probably of the West Indian race (lowland humid) and thus did not prosper in the dry climate of California. In 1871 Judge R. B. Ord obtained some cold-hardy specimens from central Mexico, and a pair of these grew well on his farm in Santa Barbara, producing copious amounts of fruit. This was the beginning of the modern avocado industry in California.

From the beginning, avocados were a profitable crop for growers. In 1905 it was reported that avocados were selling for 30 to 50 cents apiece in California. That year the average wage for the American worker was 22 cents an hour, so the avocado was truly a luxury. At roughly the same time, the British Ministry of Agriculture and Food reported that 'avocado pears' were selling in London markets at prices from one shilling to one shilling and threepence, equivalent to about £4 in 2019. Avocados in the UK must have been a treat reserved for the very well-to-do.

Avocados seemed to do well in Southern California, but until the second decade of the twentieth century, chefs who wanted to use them mostly had to import them from Mexico. The most common source was markets in the Puebla area. One of the earliest users and promoters of the avocado in the very early twentieth century was the chef of the Los

New avocado fruit.

Amanda Almira
Newton,
exterior of the
Fuerte avocado
variety, 1917.

Angeles Athletic Club. He saved the seeds of the avocados
he brought from Mexico and gave them to William Hertrich,
who grew them and used the seedlings to start an orchard
on the estate of railroad magnate Henry Huntington in San
Marino, California. The Huntington Mansion on the estate
is now the home of the Huntington Library, a famous rare
book repository. The grounds are a botanical garden, and
there are some remnants of the old orchards on the grounds.
In 1913 came the famous 'Freeze of '13', a fatal freeze that

Amanda Almira
Newton,
interior of the
Fuerte avocado
variety, 1917.

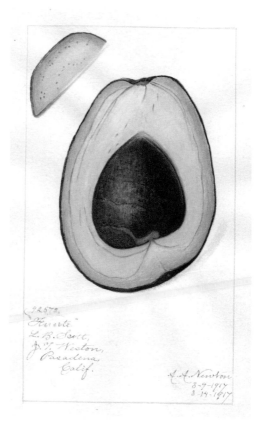

92578
"Fuerte"
L. B. Scott,
J. % Weston,
Pasadena
Calif.

A. A. Newton
8-9-1917
8-14-1917

wreaked horticultural havoc across Southern California. Avocados throughout the region were wiped out. One of the few varieties that survived and went on to thrive was the Fuerte avocado, which had been brought from Atlixco, Mexico, by the horticultural explorer Carl Schmidt.

By the beginning of the twentieth century, several avocado nurseries were operating in Southern California. The most famous of these was the West India Gardens in Altadena, where avocado legend Wilson Popenoe got his start, budding avocado trees for the owner, his father. The Popenoes thought the avocado had a bright future in California. In 1911 the elder Popenoe sent his son and one of their assistant nurserymen, Carl Schmidt, to central Mexico to gather specimens that might do well in Southern California. One of these was the Fuerte. *Fuerte*, the Spanish word for strong, was attributed to the avocado for the cold hardiness it showed in the great freeze. In 1914 a grower named John Whedon reluctantly accepted fifty Fuerte trees from Popenoe because the other varieties he had ordered had not survived the freeze. Whedon planted these young trees in Yorba Linda, California, in what became the first commercial grove of Fuerte avocados planted in the state. Whedon had great success with the Fuerte. The fruit was popular with chefs, and hotels in Los Angeles and San Francisco bought most of what he could grow at prices as high as $12 a dozen, about $8 apiece in 2019 dollars. Due to the fruit quality and the cold hardiness, he was able to sell grafting branches for $2.50, earning as much as $6,000 a year just from the scion sales.

Avocado groves in San Diego, California, early 20th century.

By 1940 the Fuerte represented 75 per cent of avocado production in California. The Fuerte was the first cultivar of significant commercial value in California and remained the standard of excellence for many years. It spread rapidly around the world and spawned the avocado industries of the Mediterranean and the Southern Hemisphere, where it remains economically important today. In California it now represents only about 2 per cent of commercial production and is seen as a niche or speciality product.

While the Fuerte is still important in the avocado industry globally, in California and Mexico it has been largely superseded by the ubiquitous Hass, now by far the number one cultivar in global commerce. The Hass avocado was a chance cross of avocados from the Mexican and Guatemalan races and was discovered by a postman in La Habra Heights, California, named Rudolph Hass. In 1926 Hass planted three seeds to serve as rootstock for a Guatemalan variety he was interested in, the Lyon. The graft succeeded on two of the trees, but not on the third. Hass ignored the third tree, but it continued to grow. He even cut it off more than once, but the tree kept coming back. Hass brought in a professional fruit grafter named Caulkins to assess his trees and to take out the non-performing rootstock. Caulkins encouraged him to let the tree grow, since it was so hardy. Soon the tree yielded an odd bumpy fruit that turned purplish-black as it ripened. The Fuerte, the most commercially successful variety at the time, was smooth and stayed green, so the new specimen did not fit the commercial expectation of the time.

For that reason Hass didn't give the odd tree much attention, but his children were crazy about the fruit. At their urging, he tried it and found it had a particularly creamy texture and a desirable nutty flavour. As the tree grew, it provided far more fruit than the family could eat, and he

92928

"Lyon" Tree 23/21

L. B. Scott

S. Pasadena, Calif.

Mary D. Arnold

4-17-17

Mary Daisy Arnold, 'Lyon' avocado variety, 1917, the type Rudolph Hass
was trying to grow when he stumbled upon the Hass.

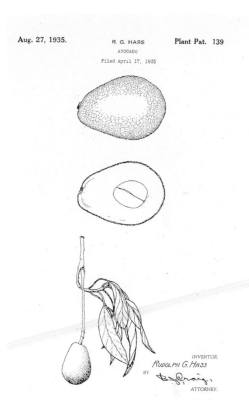

Aug. 27, 1935.   R. G. HASS   Plant Pat. 139

AVOCADO

Filed April 17, 1935

INVENTOR.
Rudolph G. Hass

BY

ATTORNEY.

began to sell the excess to his co-workers at the post office, at the Model Grocery Store in Pasadena, and eventually from a stand at the grove. The reputation of the fruit grew slowly, but ultimately it won a blue ribbon at the California State Fair. It had a high oil content (18 per cent) and the ability to hang on the tree, allowing for an extended harvest period. This, combined with the unique nutty flavour, caused other growers to become interested in it.

Rudolph Hass patented the tree in 1935 (Patent #139), making it the first tree to earn a plant patent in America. He partnered with the Brokaw Nursery in Ventura, California, to sell scions of the new tree. Though the Hass went on to become the number one avocado in the world, Hass himself earned less than $5,000 in royalties in his lifetime. The problem was that growers would buy one and then graft branches onto rootstock themselves, evading the patent fee. Hass never earned enough to quit the post office, and he died at the age of sixty in 1952, the same year the patent on the Hass avocado expired. The original Hass avocado grove in La Habra Heights was later subdivided for a housing development, and the mother tree stood in a front garden in the subdivision, where it finally died in 2002 from root rot. The tree was cut down and the wood is stored at the Brokaw Nursery, where pieces of it are occasionally used to make commemorative plaques to honour important people in the avocado industry.

California commercial avocado growers organized the California Ahuacate Association in 1915 to offer 'improvement in culture, production, and marketing' of this unique fruit. But marketing efforts and distribution were initially piecemeal and disorganized. In 1915 the association convened a meeting in one of Los Angeles's new luxury hotels, the Alexandria. The hotel was at the epicentre of the young motion picture business. Charlie Chaplin lived there for a time, and its dining room was the site of the meeting of Tom Mix, Douglas Fairbanks, Mary Pickford and D. W. Griffith that created the famous United Artists studio. Mix was said to have ridden his horse into the lobby for the meeting.

One of the first orders of business was to come up with a common name under which all growers would market the fruit. Until that time, avocados had been marketed under a variety of names, including *aguacate*, *ahuacate* and alligator pear, a practice that was felt to have impeded its commercial growth and acceptance. The growers originally thought that the Mexican name *aguacate* was the best choice, but fruit marketers objected to giving the fruit a Mexican name, given the racial climate of America in this period. They felt it would limit the market to Hispanics, who would be unable to pay the high prices the growers wanted for their fruit, and would give the fruit an unsavoury association with Mexicans, an unpopular minority group in Southern California. The growers particularly detested the 'alligator pear' moniker, thinking it too rural and rustic for a fruit they wanted to promote as upscale and luxurious. A motion was made at one of the early meetings of the California Ahuacate Association to levy a fine on any member who marketed their fruit as an alligator pear. A later release from the Avocado Growers Exchange to distributors and marketers questioned why 'the avocado, an exalted member of the laurel family should be called an alligator pear'. It continued, saying that it 'is beyond all understanding. The avocado, as a matter of fact, bears no resemblance to an alligator, a pair of alligators, or whatever the alligator mistakes for a pear. The term alligator pear is ruining the business.'

In the early twentieth century in America, the term *alligator* was used as a slang term to mean worthlessness. Someone who stole things was called an alligator. White musicians who came to black jazz clubs and stole licks and techniques from their African American counterparts were called alligators by the black players. For the marketers who wanted to sell the avocado for a premium price, allusions of worthlessness and theft would be antithetical to their purpose. This could be another reason the early California growers were so dead set against the name alligator pear.

The term 'avocado' was first adopted by the United States Department of Agriculture and the American Pomological

Society, an organization founded in 1848 to foster the commercial fruit-growing business in America. The growers at the meeting in the Alexandria Hotel in 1915 were said to have chosen this name because it sounded 'less Mexican' and more continental than *aguacate* or some of the other derivatives of *ahuacatl*. 'Avocado' was not a term that showed up in the popular dictionaries of the early twentieth century, and one of the earliest efforts of the newly rechristened California Avocado Association was to contact publishers of dictionaries and ask them to include it in future editions, noting that the plural was avocados, not avocadoes.

The first common marketing and distribution cooperative for avocados, the California Avocado Growers Exchange, was formed in 1924, and the group bought a warehouse and packing facility in Vernon, California. In 1926 they began to sell members' avocados under the brand name Calavo, and in 1927 they formally changed the name of the co-op to Calavo Growers. Currently the co-op represents about 2,600 of the largest growers in Southern California and is probably the largest non-governmental marketing force in the avocado business.

From the beginning, Calavo Growers advertised in the luxe publications of the day, such as *Vogue*, the *New Yorker* and *Vanity Fair*. Calavo Growers sent recipes to food writers around the country to promote the fruit. In an era that valued culinary sophistication, avocados were promoted for their elegant and exotic nature. The ethnic angle was downplayed and not revived until a vogue for Mexican food swept America in the 1960s and '70s. Prior to the rise of Mexican cuisine to prominence in this period, avocados remained a somewhat regional food, consumed mostly in parts of the United States that were receptive to Latin American foods.

Avocado packing plant in California, *c.* 1960.

Also gaining prominence in the 1970s was a new concept called California Cuisine. The most famous advocate of the new, fresh, local cooking style was Alice Waters, who opened her Chez Panisse restaurant in Berkeley in 1971. Other chefs soon followed her lead, and before long California was leading the way in the revolution that became the farm-to-table movement. For chefs wanting to feature foods that were close to home but unique, the avocado was a perfect fit, and it came to embody this new cuisine. Avocados were used in sandwiches and salads and as many other places as the chefs' creativity took them.

At the same time, sushi was beginning to be seen outside the Japanese enclaves of California. From the early days of the modern sushi craze, avocado has been a popular ingredient. The story goes that there was a problem getting the best fatty tuna, *toro*, and fatty tuna belly, *otoro*, in the United States and Canada. The best prices were obtained in the markets

California roll, a popular type of sushi maki roll using surimi crab and avocado.

of Japan, so most of the catch was sold there. One enterprising chef thought the buttery texture of avocados would be the best substitute for the hard-to-get tuna parts. He started using them along with surimi crab in a creation he called the California roll (which was actually invented in British Columbia – maybe he thought California had a hipper ring to it than Vancouver). The result was wildly successful and is a core product in the modern sushi repertoire.

The high price paid for avocados in the early twentieth century was a significant factor in the Southern California land boom of the 1920s. Real-estate promoters pitched the idea that anyone could move to Southern California, buy a few acres, and retire a fruit baron in just a few years. One marketing pamphlet said, 'The Avocado is more than a dessert fruit or relish. It is a Health fruit possessing unusual Vitalizing and Rejuvenating properties.' Another claimed that growing avocados would lead to a 'heritage of Health to your children in a cluster of "Green Gold"'. One brochure from

1924 calculated the yield on an acre of avocado trees and concluded that 'long before 1940 you should be on easy street'.

Prior to the Great Depression of the 1930s, agriculture was the mainstay of the California economy. The history of California during that period is one of massive marketing efforts to get California fruits into kitchens, domestic and commercial, across America. The modern American health food movement had its first big moment in the spotlight in the 1920s as real estate and commodity marketers promoted Southern California as the new land of milk and honey. Research into the vitamins and other health-giving components of foods reached a zenith in the last years of the nineteenth century and the beginning of the twentieth. In addition, large strides were being made in areas of public health such as sanitation and nutrition. Much was written in the popular press about these areas, and the topics grabbed the public imagination. Good health could be had by all if only the right foods were consumed. If the brochures were to be believed, the climate and produce of Southern California were the remedy the dyspeptic masses of America needed.

2
Growing Avocados

While most Western countries treat the avocado as a vegetable, botanically it is a fruit. Fruits are the fleshy, matured ovary of a flower that has one or more seeds. Avocados are unusual fruits in that they are neither sweet nor acidic, two of the most common traits of fruit. They also have a high level of protein and are oleaginous.

Fruits may be dry or fleshy. Nuts and legumes are examples of dry fruit. Avocados are fleshy. Fleshy fruits can be classified as drupes or berries. While the avocado meets the technical definition of a drupe (a fruit with an internally differentiated endocarp), most botanists classify the avocado as a berry because the endocarp is neither 'stiff nor stony' and is less than 2 millimetres (0.08 in.) thick. So avocados are classified as a single-seeded berry.

The avocado has one of the more complicated sex lives in the vegetable kingdom. Avocado trees have what are known as perfect flowers: that is, the flowers have both female and male characteristics. When they open on one day the flowers are all female. When they open on the following day, they are all male. Avocado trees have either A-cultivar flowers or B-cultivar flowers. A-cultivar flowers open as female on the morning of one day and as male on the afternoon of the following day. B-cultivar flowers open as female on one afternoon and as male the following morning. Growers need to have complementary A and B cultivars in proximity for the highest yields. If all the trees in an area are all from a single propagative parent – as is often the case, since about 90 per cent of the avocados grown in California and 85 per cent of those grown elsewhere are Hass – then all the flowers in the orchard may be female or male at once, reducing the chances for a vigorous fertilization.

Further complicating reproduction is the fact that avocados are dichogamous. This means that the pistils and the stamens become sexually mature at different times. If you have an orchard with various cultivars, receptive pistils should have enough pollination-ready stamens to ensure fertilization and fruit. But in today's commercial avocado orchards, where the Hass avocado is grown exclusively and all the trees are genetically identical, fruiting can be a less certain proposition. Avocado

Avocado flowers.

trees do have the potential to self-pollinate, but growers usually cannot take this chance with their livelihoods, so they use various strategies to ensure pollination.

Avocado trees are most often propagated by grafting branches from the desired parent onto rootstocks that are chosen for compatibility with local soil conditions or resistance to common pests, diseases or root rot (*phytophthora*). The plants are grown in nurseries for about a year to make sure the graft has taken, and then the trees are sold to orchardists.

The Hass avocado is by far the largest cultivar in production owing to its popularity with consumers. Fatty, creamy and vaguely nutty, the Hass has few serious challengers in the marketplace. It ships well, is small enough to be consumed in a sitting or two, has a long growing season and can stay on the tree until the grower can harvest it, and has a remarkably consistent size, shape and coloration. *Esquire* magazine calls it the Coca-Cola of avocados, the standard by which all avocados are judged. Because of this, it is unlikely the Hass will be displaced in the marketplace anytime soon. Most countries hoping to capitalize on the export of avocados will probably plant them to the exclusion of other varietals.

Of concern today is the reduction of avocado germplasm stock owing to the shrinking genetic diversity of commercial avocado production. Avocados follow the familiar pattern of certain fruit types being selected by marketers as the most desirable and the easiest to sell. As some varieties are favoured, other varieties, often heirlooms with limited growth areas or only local appeal, become endangered or even lost. As more and more growers around the world replace locally appropriate varieties with the Hass to generate revenue from exporting it, the amount of novel germplasm and genetic diversity shrinks. This could become a significant issue as the Hass becomes widely planted in the areas of Mexico where

The three stages of ripeness of the Hass avocado. Left to right green fruit; ripening; ready to eat.

the greatest reservoirs of genetic diversity reside and where the germplasm is most diverse. As avocado germplasm becomes increasingly threatened in the wild, the best new sources of it may be the trees grown from seeds by botanists and orchardists. The 'Buy Local' and 'Slow Food' movements are also attempting to slow this tendency by promoting more regionally appropriate cultivars, but progress is slow as mass-marketers are hesitant to invest in cultivars that do not have the characteristics of the Hass that make it popular with consumers. Most non-Hass varieties stay green when ripe, and consumers have been trained by the Hass avocado to expect a fruit that turns blackish-purple at the ideal stage of ripeness. But this is not an insurmountable problem. At one time the only apples in most American grocery stores were Red Delicious and Golden Delicious. Now most markets carry ten to twenty varieties of apples at any given time, and apples with different characteristics have found favour with buyers.

While there are more than five hundred recognized varieties of avocado, only a handful are grown commercially, and the Hass is by far the most widely grown of that handful. We rarely know much about the pedigree of any individual avocado cultivar. Current genetic-testing methods can tell us which of the three (or two, depending on your stance on the West Indian) races are present in any given cultivar, but beyond that, little information can be gleaned. Researchers at the University of California Extension Service say, 'Any thought of fitting today's cultivars into a concise family tree is hopelessly optimistic. Each seedling represents a reshuffled version of its parents' genomes. Contrary to many major crops, most avocado cultivars we have today are busting with so much genetic diversity that breeding is actually rendered difficult.' In today's breeding programmes, about 99 per cent of seed-grown avocado trees are discarded for not showing commercial promise, and most of the remaining 1 per cent will be culled out after further testing. Only a tiny fraction of the trees grown will show enough promise for further research. Nonetheless, avocado breeding programmes continue in hopes of

Avocado orchard in bloom, California.

Avocado
seedling.

Avocado seedling.

producing a new mega-hit, the next Hass. Mary Lu Arpaia, the head of the avocado breeding programme at the University of California, Riverside, hosts monthly tasting sessions of avocados with novel shapes, sizes and flavours with the hope of finding new varieties that can overcome some of the environmental and geographical limitations faced by avocado producers today and still find favour with consumers who have been conditioned to think that the Hass is the only acceptable form of the fruit.

Genetic modification may be the future of the avocado. To be a commercial success, avocados need to have the characteristics wanted by growers and buyers. In addition to tasting good, an avocado must have the correct texture, colour, keeping quality and ability to withstand mechanized commercial packing techniques, and it must ship well. As with most food crops, the biggest dangers to avocado crops are diseases and pests. The ubiquitous Hass is very susceptible to Fusarium dieback, a disease caused by a fungus transmitted by insects. Trees affected by the fungus have extensive branch dieback, which in turn leads to significant fruit loss. By combining genetic material from dieback-resistant varieties like the Fuerte with the eating and ripening qualities of the Hass, botanists may be able to come up with a variety that is acceptable to consumers and faces fewer issues with pests and disease in the orchard.

Orcharding of Avocados

Once established, avocado trees can be prolific producers. In a mediocre year a mature orchard can produce as many as 2,720 kilograms (6,000 lb) of avocados per acre in a season. In a year where everything happens just right, an orchard can produce as much as 5,440 kilograms (12,000 lb) an acre. A single healthy and vigorous mature avocado tree can produce as many as 4,000 fruits in a single season. When the geography and climate are just right, the avocado flourishes and is fecund. But it is fussy about temperature and moisture. Avocado trees need a frost-free climate with just the right amount of moisture. They need a lot of water to produce large and abundant fruit, but water not taken up by the tree needs to drain away quickly if root rot is to be avoided.

In places where avocados require irrigation, they drink as much as 1,700 litres (450 gallons) per week per tree. And quantity isn't the only issue. Avocados are as picky about their water as a supermodel. The Mexican race and the Guatemalan race are very sensitive to salinity of water. The West Indies race is much more salt-tolerant than the other two and may be the future of avocado cultivation as growing soils in prime growing areas like California, the Antipodes and the Mediterranean become salinized owing to extensive irrigation.

Temperature is another significant issue in avocado husbandry. Freezing temperatures and frost kill not only the fruit but the tree itself. Even if the temperature doesn't reach freezing point, many varieties will drop their fruit as the temperature nears this level. The Fuerte cultivar was the first avocado to be widely grown in California because it was the most cold-resistant variety. One reason the Hass variety replaced the Fuerte and became so widespread is that it can withstand brief, but mild, exposure to freezing temperatures.

Wind can be a big issue in avocado growing. Excessive wind is detrimental to avocado trees because it reduces the humidity level of the orchard. Avocado orchards need a certain level of humidity to function properly, especially in the flowering and pollination season. Some of the famous hot spring winds of the world like the Santa Ana of California, the Sharav

Frostbitten avocado orchard, Israel.

Young avocado grove, California.

in Israel and the berg winds in South Africa play havoc with avocado crops as they lower the humidity in some of the most productive avocado regions of the world. Strong winds also wreak destruction as avocado wood is relatively weak and brittle, and snaps easily.

Avocados are a climacteric fruit like bananas, pears and tomatoes. The fruit will ripen on the tree, but ripening is superior if it happens after the fruit is picked. Avocados that fall from the tree will begin to ripen on the ground. Thus they are picked when they are mature but not ripe. Maturity is determined by taking specific gravity readings or oil measurements. For most cultivars in commercial production a specific gravity reading of 0.96 is considered ideal. The oil measurement method is more varietal-specific, but oil content of between 5 and 15 per cent is the desired level for many commercial varieties.

One benefit that avocados offer growers is that unlike most tree fruits, the fruit can remain on the tree for many weeks after reaching maturity. This allows them to space out the harvest, which in turn helps with labour issues on a fruit that is still picked almost entirely by hand. Leaving avocado fruit on the tree too long, however, will cause it to be both stringy and rubbery, highly negative qualities in the estimation of the retail consumer. Avocados that have either of these faults tend to be sent to pulpers, who process them into guacamole and other forms. Leaving the fruit on the tree too long can also cause the tree to have a smaller crop the following year, so growers tend to harvest them as expeditiously as possible.

While avocados keep well in commercial cold storage, they tend to ripen quickly once they return to room temperature. This is because the enzymes that cause the fruit to ripen have a high rate of metabolism. Once it gets going, the fruit goes from underripe to ripe to overripe to rotten in quick procession. A company called Apeel Sciences has developed an extremely thin, semi-permeable, plant-based film (essentially invisible to the naked eye) that is sprayed

Avocados ripening in a grove.

over the skin of the avocado. The film mostly deprives the avocado of the oxygen these enzymes need to metabolize, slowing down the ripening process. An avocado thus treated can sit on the shelf longer, helping distributors and grocers with spoilage issues, though it will also take longer to ripen in the consumer's kitchen.

Owing to a property known as cell division, avocados have the ability to grow larger the longer they remain on the tree. The growth is slow after a point but does continue. An avocado will grow 300,000 times in size between fertilization and maturity. Most sellers want only small fruit, so this is not necessarily a significant advantage for the grower. But for many smallholders in less developed nations who use the avocado tree to help ensure food security, a tree that can hold its fruit and see it increase in size with little loss in quality can offer significant advantages. The weight range for most avocado cultivars is between 113 grams (4 oz) and 1.8 kilograms (4 lb). The world's largest avocado, weighing over 3.6 kilograms (8 lb) was found in Hawaii. The avocado is known for the size of its stone, and the seed makes up about 10 to 25 per cent of the weight of an avocado depending on the cultivar.

The newest market form of avocado is the cocktail avocado. Sold by merchants such as the British supermarket Marks & Spencer during the winter holiday season, it is an elongated fruit 5 to 8 centimetres (2–3 in.) long. It has no stone and is 100 per cent edible, including the skin. This is a sexually immature avocado that results when the fruit doesn't develop a seed as it grows. Once they get to the size where they would normally begin to develop a stone, they stop growing. They are known as cukes in the avocado trade and usually were discarded in the orchard as valueless. Now they are gleaned and marketed as cocktail avocados, and

Seedless cocktail avocado with regularly sized fruits.

sold for a premium price. *The Independent* newspaper in the UK offered up cocktail avocados as a way to reduce the incidence of 'avocado hand', a condition seen more and more in hospitals as people cut avocados in their hands instead of on a cutting board. Increasing numbers of people arriving at the emergency department with this condition has led the British Association of Plastic, Reconstructive and Aesthetic Surgeons to call for safety warning labels to be placed on avocados. The most famous victim of this condition was Meryl Streep, who showed off her wound at a panel discussion in the Apple Store in New York City in 2012.

Avocados are picked when mature and held or shipped at just under 4°C (40°F), which retards further ripening until they get to the merchant, who sets them out at room temperature, whereupon the ripening process recommences. Some merchants, especially wholesalers selling to end-point users, use a 'ripening room' where ethylene gas is pumped in to speed-ripen avocados, so they are available for immediate use. Most restaurants and grocery store consumers want fruit they can consume immediately. The eating quality of an avocado – that is, the creaminess of the flesh and the oiliness of the mouthfeel – is best if it is picked as soon as it is gauged to be mature. Picking them at the earliest possible moment after they meet a maturity standard also helps them stand up to post-harvest processing and shipping owing to their firmness.

The Ecology of Avocado Production

The temperate forests and rolling hills of Michoacán are ideal avocado country. This beautiful region, with its hillsides of porous volcanic soil, is ideally suited for growing avocados. It gets enough rainfall during the moist six months of the year that the orchards of the region need little irrigation. The pine forests are largely self-regenerating and act as a giant carbon sink for the entire region. The rolling nature of the land and the traditional agricultural patterns of the region make it an ideal place for the smallholder to make a living. The average size of an orchard here, while growing, is still small, and many growers are making a living on a plot of 10 hectares (25 acres) or less. Avocado production, packing and distribution provides more than 300,000 jobs in a place where employment can be irregular.

But there is trouble in paradise. While there are about 150,000 hectares (370,000 acres) of legal, registered and monitored avocado orchards in Michoacán, there are probably another 50,000 hectares (123,000 acres) of illegal, unregistered and unmonitored orchards. There are also many more unregistered orchards in the neighbouring states of Jalisco, Colima, Mexico and Morelos. The official policy of the Mexican Ministry of Agriculture, Livestock, Rural Development, Fisheries, and Food, known by the acronym SAGARPA, is to encourage the development of avocado orchards as a way to promote economic development in poorer rural regions of Mexico. But unintended consequences of this policy have caused harm to the regional ecology.

One of the most devastating effects has been the impact on groundwater. To plant orchards, growers often displace the native pine forest. Avocado trees tend to take up nearly all the water that comes to their roots, as opposed to pine trees, which take a small amount and allow the rest to pass by and into the water table. One mature avocado tree uses as much water as fourteen mature pine trees. This negatively impacts runoff and groundwater recharge. Drinking water wells and irrigation wells in the areas around avocado orchards have been negatively impacted by avocado orcharding efforts. Small streams in these areas that once ran year-round are now seasonal. The change from coniferous to deciduous trees has affected micro-climatic patterns in these areas, and rainfall now tends to be concentrated in the summer months of June, July and August, whereas before it was spread more evenly throughout the six-month rainy season.

The unquenchable American thirst for avocados is also endangering the monarch butterfly. Michoacán is a stop on the migration route for many monarchs, which migrate thousands of kilometres from Canada and the U.S. to winter homes in the forests of Michoacán and Guerrero. The prime wintering habitat for the butterfly is oyamel fir trees in the two states. The pine and oak forests in this area provide the monarch with the food it needs to overwinter. As more and more forest is converted to avocado orchards, it becomes harder for these magnificent creatures to get the food they need to overwinter. The Mexican government has designated over 80,000 hectares (200,000 acres) of these pine-oak forests as monarch preserves, but enforcement is hard and avocado orchards continue to creep into the preserves. Monarch tourism is on the upswing and this may save the forests from total encroachment by illegal avocado orchards.

Greenpeace Mexico, commenting on the ecological situation in Michoacán, has said, 'Beyond the displacements of forests and the effects on water retention, the high levels of agricultural chemicals used on the trees and the large volumes of wood needed to pack and ship avocados are other factors that could have negative effects on the area's environment and the well-being of its inhabitants.' Anecdotal evidence suggests that cancer rates are rising in Mexico's avocado

Overwintering monarch butterflies.

production zones and children in schools near orchards report having lung and stomach problems, health issues commonly associated with high levels of farm chemical use.

Methods used to clear land for avocado production in Mexico are problematic as well. Mexican government officials estimate that 40 per cent of forest fires in avocado-growing areas are the result of the methods used to clear land of pines in order to plant avocado orchards. Every year, another 20,000 hectares (49,000 acres) of wild forest are cleared to plant avocados. The need to have labour at hand for the orchards has also resulted in the creation of many small towns in what were formerly wild forestlands, with associated negative environmental impacts.

While almonds have long been the poster child for extravagant agricultural water use, avocados usually require just as much water to produce a pound of fruit. On average it takes a bathtub full of water to produce one avocado fruit. The amount of water used to grow the avocados currently consumed in the UK is equal to the amount it would take to fill 12,000 Olympic-sized swimming pools. In Michoacán, it only takes 113 litres (30 gallons) of water to produce every ½ kilogram (1 lb) of fruit, and little of this is irrigation water. In California, growers use about 284 litres (75 gallons) of water for every ½ kilogram (1 lb) of avocados they produce. Most of this water is imported into the growing areas from regions that are water-starved as a result. In Chile, an up-and-coming producer, the ratio is nearly 378 litres of water (100 gallons) per ½ kilogram (1 lb) of fruit produced, and nearly all of it is irrigation water. As a result, global avocado production is shifting to areas where less irrigation water is needed to produce the fruit. Growers in California are increasingly uprooting orchards and replacing them with crops that are less water-intensive, such as strawberries and grapes. Production is

creasingly shifting to countries where rainfall can provide
ost of the trees' water needs, such as Indonesia, Kenya and
mbabwe, where on average the irrigation need is about 94
ded litres (25 gallons) of water per ½ kg (1 pound).

The problems associated with water use and avocados are
ecially problematic in Chile, a growing source of the fruit
in export markets. Groundwater is supposed to be a public
resource in Chile, but so much of it has been appropriated
by avocado ranchers that many smallholders around large
orchards have had to abandon their farms. Avocado growing
in Chile is an especially thirsty business. Arid conditions in the
prime growing areas means that an avocado grown in Chile
uses nearly three times as much water as one grown in places
like Mexico and the Dominican Republic.

Groundwater is prone to theft in Chile because there is
virtually no governmental regulation of its distribution, a
policy holdover from the days of the Pinochet government
(1973–90). Under President Pinochet, large landowners were
given carte blanche to use as much groundwater as they
wanted. The deep wells that avocado growers have drilled to
water their orchards have left the wells of smallholders and
local rivers dry. Activists advocating for smallholders in the
affected areas describe once-thriving areas as ghost valleys,
deprived of all population not required to grow or harvest
avocados.

Legislation to stem groundwater depletion has been
introduced in the Chilean Senate but continues to be held up
by the large landowners. The large landowners and avocado
growers argue that increasing capture, that is, building large
reservoirs, is the answer to the problem, and they advocate for
that solution. There is a National Irrigation Commission in
Chile, but it does not have the resources to adequately monitor
water flow from irrigation wells. Water activists are calling for

the nationalization of all of Chile's freshwater sources to ensure more equitable distribution of the water. But large landowners and companies that control the packing, sale and export of avocados and other agricultural goods still hold immense political power, and the issue is far from settled.

One solution that has been proposed to help reduce the huge thirst of the avocado is genetic modification. The hope is that trees can be developed that grow with less water and accept irrigation water with a higher level of salinity. But this will be tricky for the avocado industry as one of the key marketing propositions for avocados is health. Customers who are health-conscious look for clean labels, organic foods and, above all, non-genetically modified food items. These consumers will probably recoil at the idea of a genetically modified avocado based on the acceptance levels of genetically modified fruits and vegetables that have been test marketed already.

Most exported avocados are consumed far from where they are produced. Given their propensity to begin ripening when exposed to oxygen, most avocados are transported by air from where they are grown. Britain is one of the largest markets for New Zealand avocados, but environmental groups estimate that each New Zealand avocado sold in a UK grocery generates nearly a metric tonne and a half of carbon emissions.

Climate change, or global warming, will be a problem for the avocado business. Avocados could once again become luxury items if climate change raises temperatures significantly in growing areas. Researchers from the Lawrence Livermore Laboratory in California estimate that even a mild temperature rise in avocado-growing areas will reduce crop yields by as much as 40 per cent. This could be especially devastating in areas already operating in the high end of avocado comfort ranges such as Australia. Heatwaves on the Mornington

An Avocado seller in Uganda.

Peninsula outside Melbourne, a large avocado-growing area, have already wiped out entire growing seasons.

There are some bright spots on the horizon for sustainable avocado production. Peru is another South American country that has become a significant exporter. Rich, sandy soils and a consistent water flow from the Andes combined with a near-ideal climate make Peru a good location for avocado cultivation and efforts are being made there to ensure that avocado production remains sustainable. The most stringent environmental practices are in Israel, where avocados are grown with drip irrigation and other eco-sensitive methods. In Michoacán, Equal Exchange, a U.S./UK cooperative dedicated to helping small farmers in less-developed nations get better prices for commodities like cacao and coffee, has started an avocado project. Called PRAGOR, it is a collective of smallholders who produce organic avocados using sustainable practices. PRAGOR's members run their own farms and participate together in the packing and marketing of their avocados.

The vogue for organic fruit extends to avocados and more avocados are being produced this way. Both Mexico and California have seen a rise in the number of operations that are certified as organic. In Mexico farmers interested in sustainability have created integrated avocado operations where avocado growing and swine culture are combined. Pigs are reared on the fruit considered unsuitable for the market, and their manure is used to fertilize the trees in the orchard. Organic avocados are available in most markets. In the UK a Soil Association sticker is placed on avocados that meet British sustainable farming standards.

Peru and the Dominican Republic are the best bets for the future of sustainable avocado production. Peru is actively working to place the orchards in the areas of least ecological sensitivity and easiest access to water. The Dominican Republic, like Michoacán, is a country where avocados can thrive with a minimum of intervention. The Dominican Republic has a favourable climate, a hilly upland geography, good soil and adequate water. The biggest obstacle facing Dominican growers is that the varieties that do best there

Greenskin avocado of the West Indian Type.

are green-skin Caribbean types and not the Hass cultivar favoured by most marketers. Israel has the potential to be a leading sustainable grower, but the hilly areas in which the avocado does best have regular frost problems that play havoc with the crop. The amount of land in Israel that is perfect for avocados is limited, so that country may never become more than a niche provider.

The United States could be a good choice for sustainable growing, as prices would support it and there is a great interest in clean labels by consumers, but labour issues are causing growers to switch to crops that use less labour to pick by hand or that can be picked entirely by machines. A tight and expensive labour market combined with the increasing price of irrigation water is making avocado production increasingly expensive in the u.s., and the profitability of the crop is diminished with each passing year. There could be a time in the relatively near future where avocado production in the U.S. is limited to boutique production of organic or heirloom varietals.

Global Avocado Production

The avocado is grown commercially on at least a domestic scale in 64 countries, according to the Food and Agriculture Organization of the United Nations. Since this number only considers places where avocados are grown for resale, it probably omits a few countries where the avocado is grown for sustenance purposes by smallholders. This means that avocados are grown in nearly a third of the countries on the planet and on every continent except Antarctica. In 2016 world producers agreed to the formation and funding of the World Avocado Organization to promote avocados from

Offloading the avocado crop, Kenya.

RANK	NATION
1	Mexico
2	Dominican Republic
3	Peru
4	Indonesia
5	Colombia
6	Kenya
7	United States
8	Rwanda
9	Chile
10	Brazil

Top avocado-producing nations.

all global sources. This group mainly promotes avocados in non-North American markets where consumption is growing, such as the European Union and East Asia.

Countries in Latin America are the dominant avocado producers globally. Mexico is the largest producer, with no other country coming close. In most years, Mexico grows nearly 1.5 million tonnes of the green gems, and exports nearly half of the avocados consumed globally. Together, the major producers of the Americas, including Mexico, Peru, Chile, the Dominican Republic and Colombia, account for 71 per cent of the avocados grown in the world.

In a short time, the Dominican Republic has become one of world's largest producers of the fruit, second only to Mexico, producing some 363,000 metric tonnes a year (400,000 tons). However, domestic consumption is so high that the country ranks only twelfth among avocado exporters. The second-largest exporter of avocados is Peru, with Chile occupying third place. In Europe the primary producer and exporter is Spain, and in the Middle East the largest exporter is Israel. In the Southern Hemisphere, New Zealand has surpassed South Africa as the largest exporter, but Indonesia has planted significant acreage, most of it aimed at the export market, and it should soon surpass New Zealand.

America produces lots of avocados, nearly $500 million worth a year, but virtually all of them are consumed domestically, with a tiny trickle heading north to Canadian markets. In addition to the 117,000 metric tonnes (129,000 tons) of fruit grown in California, another 45,300 metric tonnes (50,000 tons) are produced in Florida, Texas, Arizona, Hawaii and other states. Despite being one of the larger producers of avocados, the u.s. is also one of the largest importers, buying about three times as much foreign product as it grows domestically. One reason is the limited growing range of the fruit in Southern California. In addition, there are several months a year when orchards in California will not produce fruit.

Indonesian avocado wholesaler – Banda Aceh.

While the Americas represent the lion's share of avocado production, the profitability of the avocado trade has started a 'green rush' around the world. The amount of hard currency avocado exports can bring to a less-developed nation is hard to resist. In addition to the export value of the crop, the avocado can provide nutrition locally. In fact, most of the countries that grow avocados commercially export less than 10 per cent of their crop, consuming the remainder domestically. Between the two values, the number of places where the avocado is grown continues to increase.

Avocado production has become widespread in countries with favourable climates on both sides of the equator. Southeast Asian nations have embraced the avocado enthusiastically and grow for both the export market and domestic

Leaf and fruit of Maluma avocado, a South African cultivar.

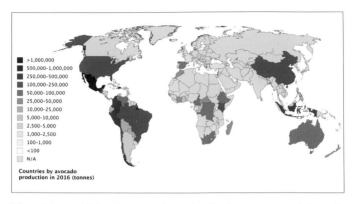

Map of the world showing avocado production by country, 2016. Central America and South America lead the way in production.

consumption. Large producers include Indonesia, Vietnam, Malaysia and the Philippines. Sub-Saharan Africa is the new frontier in avocado production as countries seek to take advantage of climates that are favourable to avocado production. South Africa was the first sub-Saharan African nation to grow avocados, but persistent drought has made long-term prospects for avocado growing on a commercial scale questionable. Countries with more reliable rainfall and humidity levels, such as Rwanda, Kenya, Swaziland and Madagascar, are rushing to fill the gap left by the decline of the South African avocado industry. Avocado consumption in China is growing rapidly, but currently all avocados are imported, mostly from Chile. However, nearly 2,000 hectares (5,000 acres) have been planted to test the potential for the tree in China, and there are plans to increase this number exponentially if the experiment succeeds. In Europe Spain is by far the number one grower, with Portugal a distant second, followed by Greece and Cyprus. Avocados are a significant cash crop for Israel and most wind up in European markets.

Global Consumption of Avocados

Who eats avocados? Nearly everyone, at least if social media is to be believed. Guacamole and avocado toast appear to be the top foods on photo-sharing apps, and consumption shows no signs of decline. The countries that grow the most avocados – Mexico, the Dominican Republic and the United States – are also the largest consumers of avocados, growing and eating about 40 per cent of world production. Citizens of the Dominican Republic eat a whopping 48 kilograms (105 lb) of the green fruit per capita, dwarfing the per capita consumption of the nearest followers, Costa Rica and Israel, at 8.1 kilograms (17.8 lb) and 7.6 kilograms (16.7 lb) respectively. Americans eat around 4 kilograms (9 lb) a year, a threefold increase since 2000 and a per capita number that is particularly impressive given that the U.S. population grew by 41 million people in the same period. Europeans eat about 1 kilogram (2.2 lb) a year, with the French being the largest consumers in Europe. Europe is the second-largest consumer market for avocados after the United States. Spain, the largest European producer, and the United Kingdom each consume slightly less than 1 kilogram a year per capita, but the consumption rate is climbing steadily in both countries. Across the world, most countries have at least tripled their avocado consumption since 2000, and consumption rates remain robust.

At one time Mexico, the largest producer of avocados in the world, was also the leader in consumption, more than 21 kilograms (46 lb) a year per capita at its peak. Now the average Mexican eats only 6.1 kilograms (13.5 lb) a year, and that number is declining. In some food markets in Mexico a large, good-quality avocado now sells for about the equivalent of Mexico's legal minimum daily wage. Ordinary Mexicans have effectively been priced out of the avocado market.

Mexican orchards now produce mainly Hass avocados, the favourite in avocado-importing countries. While Mexico still produces more avocados than any other country in the world, accounting for nearly half of the avocados in international trade, more and more are being shipped out of the country as export goods. People in other parts of North America, the main Mexican export market, pay so much more for the fruit that Mexican growers prefer to supply the foreign market rather than the domestic one.

Mexico is also the largest exporter of prepared avocado products. Peeled avocado halves are frozen with liquid nitrogen, vacuum packed, and shipped and stored frozen. These can then be thawed and used as you would fresh avocados, for slicing and dicing. Guacamole, made from second- and third-grade fruits, is the largest-volume processed avocado food item exported from Mexico.

In the u.s., what probably started the current avocado consumption boom was the loosening of the avocado import ban in 1997. Since the early part of the twentieth century, the American avocado lobby had been able to keep out all imports on the notion that Mexican pests would infest American orchards. But demand for avocados in America was growing past what California and Florida could provide. The Mexican government used this clamour for more avocado availability in the u.s. to demand their rights under the North American Free Trade Agreement (NAFTA) to be able to freely sell agricultural products to their trading partners, the u.s. and Canada, though it should be noted that the u.s. capitulated only after Mexico threatened to shut its markets to American corn, one of the most profitable agricultural crops in the u.s. After Americans could get all the (relatively) affordable avocados they wanted, consumption quadrupled over the following decade. The 1980s and '90s were also a period of increased immigration into the U.S. by people from Mexico and Central America, who already would have been regular consumers of avocados.

America is not the only place where avocado consumption is on the rise. Nielsen Research reported that avocados were the third-fastest-growing food product in the UK in 2017, led only by Budweiser beer and Monster Energy Drinks and ahead of Coca-Cola and Barefoot Wines. Avocado consumption in the United Kingdom is growing quickly, and most high-street sandwich chains feature avocado, usually in the form of guacamole, as an available ingredient. Pret A Manger offers avocado as an option on about a third of its sandwiches and wraps and uses nearly 15,000 avocados a day in its UK operations. Avocados have been available in Britain for centuries, but it was only in the 1960s that interest in the fruit became widespread. In the UK the avocado had a reputation as a winter fruit, since most avocados came from places where the crop matured in the autumn and was sent to UK markets around the first of the year. As production took hold in the Southern Hemisphere, exports from traditional UK trade partners such as South Africa and New Zealand made the fruit available year-round. While some fruit comes from the Antipodes, most of the avocados consumed in the UK come from Spain, Israel and South Africa, with a smaller number coming from Peru and Chile.

In an attempt to assert that they were Britain's most innovative food retailer, Marks & Spencer ran an advertisement featuring 1960s supermodel Twiggy claiming it had introduced the avocado to the UK in 1968. Sainsbury's shot back that it had been selling them as early as 1962, and the British press happily reported on the 'Avocado War' between the two companies. As Violet Henderson, a writer for British *Vogue* Britain, pointed out, avocados have been available off and on

Avocado, from the 'Fruits' series for the Allen & Ginter Cigarettes brand, 1891.

in Britain since the 1700s and neither store could take credit for the introduction. Certainly, they were available enough by the mid-1960s for the 1966 edition of *Mrs Beeton's Cookery and Household Management* to suggest them for sophisticated entertaining.

Avocado consumption is increasing in other countries as their middle classes continue to grow, with their members gaining a disposable income. In China, the fastest-growing market, avocado consumption is seen as a desirable badge of the adoption of a Western-informed, middle-class lifestyle. In 2017 the 5,000 stores of the KFC chain in China planned a

Avocado crate art for King Salad.

three-week-long avocado promotion. The chain offered a spicy fried chicken patty sandwich topped with avocado. It was so popular that the promotion had to end early as the stores ran out of avocados. The consumption of avocados in China has created such a demand that marketers are beginning to sell #2 grade avocados, formerly sent directly to processors, to food-service providers who don't need visually perfect whole fruit.

The Dark Side of Avocados

Michoacán is a verdant, Mediterranean-like landscape in central Mexico. Sitting about 320 kilometres (200 mi.) west of the capital, Mexico City, it has always been the centre of Mexican avocado production. Volcanic eruptions have left the hillsides exceptionally fertile, and the combination of the climate, soil and altitude makes Michoacán an ideal place for avocado growing. While the state has citrus orchards, timber plantations and even marijuana fields, the largest cash crop by far is avocados. About 90 per cent of Mexican production comes from Michoacán.

America banned imports of Mexican avocados from 1915 until 1993. In 1993 avocados were permitted to be sold in cold-weather states well away from u.s. avocado production areas, and the geographic restrictions on where Mexican avocados could be sold in the u.s. got progressively looser over the following decade. Once Mexican avocados were allowed in the u.s. market, avocado production grew by more than 50 per cent and exports rose nearly fivefold in just over a decade.

The lifting of the ban and the increased production fed what has been dubbed 'the green rush'. Avocados went from being a cheap local staple to a billion-dollar export business virtually overnight. At the height of the boom, 1 hectare (2.5 acres) of orchard, producing two crops a year, could produce avocados selling for as much as $100,000. Growers dubbed them *oro verde* – green gold. Within a few years avocados were the largest cash crop in the region, much more valuable than the previous *oro verde*, marijuana. Farmers who came from families that had been tenant farmers and *campesinos* for generations suddenly found themselves in the middle class.

The amount of money to be made from the avocado business attracted not only the *campesinos*, but the criminal element as well. The avocado boom of the 1990s coincided with one of Mexico's periodic crackdowns on organized crime. Crime bosses and *narcotraficantes* were looking for ways to keep their cash flow coming as the government curtailed their illegal drug activities. They looked around and liked what they saw in the avocado orchards of Michoacán.

As *narcotraficantes* are wont to do in Mexico, in addition to dominating the drug trade in the area they control, they try to preside over and exploit, either directly or indirectly, profitable local industries. In Michoacán this meant the avocado trade, by far the largest industry in the region. To aid in this process, the drug cartels in Mexico use a policy called 'silver or lead' to influence governmental officials. An official is first offered 'the silver', a substantial bribe. If it is refused, then they (or a family member) are killed, usually quite publicly, as a message to others: 'the lead'.

The first drug cartel to seize on the opportunities presented by the avocado business in Michoacán was *La Familia*, 'the Family'. The leader of *La Familia* was a former minister named Nazario Moreno who was known to quote Bible verses to justify the kidnapping and execution of anyone he felt threatened his power or turf. *La Familia* was running the marijuana business in Michoacán when the avocado green rush began, and the cartel quickly moved in on the legitimate avocado business. In 2010 Moreno was killed in one of Mexico's many disputes between drug cartels. After a period in which various groups vied for control of the region's criminal activities, a group called the *Caballeros Templarios*, the Knights Templar, emerged as the victors.

In Michoacán suborned public officials provided the Knights Templar with land records about the avocado growers and the size of their holdings. The cartel then 'taxed' the growers – about $100 a year for each hectare of orchard, plus a few cents for each kilogram of avocado production. Growers who refused to pay the tax were dealt with like governmental officials. (If they refused 'the silver', they were given 'the lead'.) Those who were deemed obstreperous had their orchards burned and their families terrorized. Growers who abandoned their orchards to escape the terror were forced to sign the land over to members of the Knights Templar.

As time passed and the avocado industry grew, the cartel forced its way into the avocado packing and shipping businesses as well. These businesses, often with American corporate owners or partners, paid a tax on every pound of avocados they packed and shipped. Companies that provided roving picking crews paid a head tax of a few dollars per employee per year. Some municipalities were extorted to turn over a percentage of their municipal budget as a tribute to the Knights. Revenues from these activities were estimated to run as high as a quarter of a billion dollars a year. By the mid-2010s the Knights Templar were the largest single business entity in the state of Michoacán. The cartel was estimated to have direct ownership of about 10 per cent of the orchards in the state and indirect control of a much larger percentage.

By 2014 some farmers had begun to fight back. Some towns and grower groups began to organize armed militias know as *auto-defensas*. These militias patrolled towns, roads and rural areas and fought against the cartels. Some militias were successful enough to be able to return control of some orchards to their rightful owners. In the face of this success, some of the militias were officially recognized as police forces and were armed and supported by the Mexican army. But success was localized and spotty. Cartels continue to control certain areas in the region.

In the town of Tancítaro in far-western Michoacán, avocado producers created their own militia called the Public Security Corps, known locally by its acronym CUSEPT. Members of CUSEPT are uniformed officers who wear body armour and carry high-power weaponry. They patrol the hilly orchard country around the town and have checkpoints set up along highways to deter the cartels from engaging in theft and extortion. They operate on a voluntary donation system from local growers and receive a subsidy from the Mexican government. Locals seem to be supportive of the effort, and the town is calmer and appears more prosperous than similar towns under the control of the cartels.

While Tancítaro is a success story, the effectiveness of *auto-defensas* waxes and wanes. In response to the wave of early successes by the *auto-defensas*, most cartels lowered their taxes considerably in a bid to retain control of the business.

Tancítaro, Mexico.

For some growers, this lower rate of taxation was acceptable and accommodation with the cartels was made. In other areas the militias have been subverted by the cartels to put a veneer of respectability on their activities. One of these sanitized efforts is led by the H3 cartel, a gang named after the Hummer vehicle model popular with *narcotraficantes*. Once government-sponsored, it now operates outside the governmental structure for militias, but maintains it is an official anti-trafficker militia.

The Knights Templar were largely broken up when their leader, Servando Gomez, was arrested on drug charges in 2015, but this led to another regional drug war whose eventual victors were a cartel from the neighbouring state of Jalisco known as *Nuevo Generacion*, the New Generation. They operate much as the Knights Templar did, though they attempt to position themselves as modern-day Robin Hoods who take from the rich and give to the poor. To this end, they often fund schools, hospitals and private welfare systems in the areas they control. The New Generation cartel was described as one of the most brutal *narcotraficante* organizations by United States Attorney General Jeff Sessions in 2018. Another group, known as *Los Viagros*, a backhanded reference to the stand-on-end hairstyle of its leader, have effective control of many highways in Michoacán, charging road tolls to truck drivers of agricultural products, primarily avocados and citrus fruit. The Mexican army has made concerted efforts to free the roads from gang control, but the work has not been 100 per cent successful and governmental control is not consistent.

3
Selling an Odd,
but Nutritious, Fruit

The selling of the avocado is an interesting chapter in the annals of fruit and vegetable marketing. In the beginning there was no real demand for this odd fruit. Growers planted the fruit, then had to figure out how to sell it. It was truly a case of build it and (we hope) they will come. Avocados are so ubiquitous today that we forget it took decades of dedicated and creative marketing to make them a universal little luxury.

Finding the avocado variety that would appeal to the masses took decades of experimentation, and it was nearly eighty years into the process that the true saviour of the industry, the Hass avocado, began to hit the shelves. The avocado was a hard sell because it didn't fit into any of the neat categories of the Euro-American culinary repertoire. It's a fruit, but it isn't sweet. It isn't ready to eat straight from the market (at least not until very recently). It should be eaten raw and has never really been seen as dessert by Europeans and Americans. For much of its modern history, the avocado has had to battle its image as fatty and energy-dense. In America it seemed distinctly foreign, which made it a harder sell to people who took one hundred years to accept spaghetti as a normal dinner. It was not considered a manly food and was seen as both feminine and the province of the elite. In Europe acceptance was even slower, as it was not a regular component of the diet of any ethnic group of the continent. Early marketers targeted upper- and middle-class women with their efforts since they had the monetary resources to afford a relatively expensive fruit and acted as gatekeepers for the food that entered the home.

One issue that American marketers had to contend with in the early days was the association of avocados with Mexicans and Mexican food. Even without factoring in racial prejudice, which was significant, most Americans who didn't live near the border with Mexico were simply unfamiliar with Mexican food. The days of having a Taco Bell or Chipotle in every strip mall were far in the future. Today consumers around the globe regularly eat tacos, burritos and other foods from the Latin repertoire, but in the first half of the twentieth century most Americans had only the vaguest concept of the food that was eaten by their neighbours to the south, if they had any idea at all.

Faced with the need to find a bridge into the consciousness of affluent white consumers, marketers decided to make the avocado an aspirational food, luxurious and elegant. Print advertising (the dominant medium of the period) for avocados, as with many other foods, often included recipes so consumers would know how to correctly use the fruit. To make a connection with glamorous lifestyles, the recipes

Avocado crate art for Golden Hours.

often paired the avocado with other luxury or exotic foods such as lobster or grapefruit.

Early marketers also had to contend with avocado's reputation as an aphrodisiac in early twentieth-century America. At that time you couldn't market a fruit as sexy. The Jazz Age had certainly stretched what was tolerable in society, but it hadn't been stretched as far as a sexy fruit advertisement. Even the relatively tame Miss Chiquita Banana didn't make her debut until the end of the First World War. The growers may or may not have been prudes themselves, but they wanted the approach to marketing avocados to be circumspect. Privately, marketers thought that the aphrodisiacal reputation of the avocado would be its strongest selling point. So what the ingenious marketers did was to issue a statement that avocados were absolutely, definitely, NOT an aphrodisiac. As Waverley Root said in *Eating in America* (1976), avocado growers 'deny with indignation the false and malicious rumors that the avocado was aphrodisiac'. Sales improved almost immediately.

While marketing to the elite and the status seeker was a good strategy for a minor crop, it wouldn't do if the avocado were to become a mass-market commodity. An advertising executive told the Avocado Commission to think about the example of broccoli, a food that had followed a similar marketing and acceptance path. In the beginning broccoli was novel and exotic and only served in the nicer places. As an early adman related to a meeting of the California Avocado Society, 'It got around that broccoli was a smart thing to serve on menus. It suddenly appeared on the menus of fashionable restaurants. Few people knew just what it was or where it came from, but thousands of people began wanting broccoli because it was the new and proper thing to serve.' The trick was now to do this for avocados.

While avocado growth was slow in the years after the First World War, it did benefit from a renewed interest in dietary health coming to the fore in the interwar years. Food-related editorial and advertising content in popular newspapers and magazines was heavy on dietary advice. The earliest marketing efforts based on dietary benefit offered the avocado as an antidote to the American diet of too much salt, fatty meat and gravy. Most stomach issues and digestive troubles were thought to be caused by this terrible diet. The remedy, according to the marketers? A diet teeming with fresh California produce with an avocado at the centre of the plate. As would happen again in the 1970s and the early twenty-first century, the avocado was declaimed the perfect food. Professor John Eliot Coit told the California Avocado Society in a speech in 1928:

> The American citizen is giving more thought to the effect of different foods on his complexion, his digestion, his elimination. Popular magazines are filled with articles on foods as well as advertisements of foods. The science of dietetics is booming. A man's stomach is only so large. He now emphasizes quality rather than quantity. He seeks to avoid acidosis, constipation, and corpulency. He takes great satisfaction in the new menu of fruits and salads and fresh juices. He is revolting from a diet of meat and highly milled grains, and welcomes a salad fruit. The avocado, being the aristocrat of salad fruits, fits precisely into this trend of the times . . . Rest assured that from now on the citizen is going to have a fresh salad with his hog and hominy.

Marketing of avocados is done by state, regional and national boards. The largest marketer of avocados in the world is Calavo, which markets and distributes virtually all of the California crop and a good deal of the Mexican fruit imported to the United States. Florida avocados are represented by a group called Flavacado, a play on the name of the state and the flavourful nature of the fruit. In Mexico the marketing board is called Avocados from Mexico and performs a similar function. These organizations spend millions to promote the product in various media. These commissions are usually funded by a per-pound fee that growers pay when they have the boards distribute their product.

UK food researcher Anne Murcott says that avocados are a good example of how modern food marketing works. First you work at creating a buzz for the product; touting it as a superfood helps a lot here. You back this up by having the product in the market and at food service establishments as you turn up the marketing. You spend a lot on marketing in

Avocados in the market, Da Lat, Vietnam.

Avocado toast with purple flowers.

traditional media and put it out on social media constantly. All of this increases demand at both the retail and wholesale level. If you manage to get a hit, the money rolls in. Avocado marketers managed to do all of this exactly right. The combination of a devoted and decades-long marketing effort, the relaxation of imports to the U.S. owing to NAFTA obligations, the global spread of quick service chains willing to use it on their menus, the growing interest in so-called 'superfoods', and the photogenic nature of the avocado in a world obsessed with social media: all of these created a perfect storm for the odd fruit that seemed not to fit into any known niche. The avocado also has benefited from the fact that it is somewhat immune to substitution. One leafy green is much like another. If kale gets too expensive it can be replaced with another green like spinach or collards. The same applies to grains. If quinoa becomes expensive or hard to obtain, there is always teff or faro, or one could even fall back on brown rice. But there is really nothing else quite like the avocado in the vegetable kingdom. After years of dogged marketing, its nutritional profile, flavour and social cachet have marked the avocado as the premier badge of social hipness.

One of the best moves made by American marketers was to associate guacamole with America's most popular sporting event, the Super Bowl. Starting with a Guacamole Bowl advert in 1992 where players and their families competed to have their guacamole declared the winner, to a series of creative adverts touting guacamole as the ultimate game day food, the American and Mexican marketing boards have made guacamole as American as apple pie. Avocados were the first fruit to be advertised during the Super Bowl with an ad that cost $4.5 million. Americans now consume over 45 million kilograms (100 million lb) of avocados on Super Bowl Sunday, most of it in the form of guacamole. Another 41 million kilograms (90 million lb) is consumed on Cinco de Mayo, the Mexican holiday that is celebrated more widely in the United States than in its home country. While the u.s. still imports more kilograms of pineapples, bananas and strawberries, the dollar value of avocado imports is higher than all three of them.

Given the extreme popularity of avocados at the beginning of the twenty-first century, it is no surprise that municipal

Avocado plush toy.

governments are using avocado festivals to drive the tourist trade. There are avocado festivals in the places where you would expect them, such as Carpenteria and Fallbrook, both in the California avocado belt, and in Uruapan and Tancítaro, Mexico, both claiming to be the Avocado Capital of the World (though this claim is made by Fallbrook as well). But there are also avocado festivals in quite unexpected places. New Caledonia, in the South Pacific, holds a major avocado festival in late April or early May. In September the quaintly named Australian town of Blackbutt, Queensland, holds its avocado festival. The Fallbrook Avocado Festival claims to be the world's oldest avocado festival, having been celebrated annually since at least 1985. It has a Best Guacamole recipe contest, a Little Miss and Mister Avocado Pageant, an 'Art of the Avocado' contest with both 2-D and 3-D categories, and the Avocado 500, where contestants make a model-sized race car from an avocado and race against other entrants. The Carpenteria festival, with the tag line 'Peace, Love, and Avocados', is billed as the largest free fair in Southern California and one of the largest in the United States.

Avocado Rustling

Given how valuable the avocado is, avocado theft, or avocado rustling as newspapers like to call it, should come as no surprise. As early as the 1970s, both the *New York Times* and the *Los Angeles Times*, as well as *Time* magazine, were printing articles on avocado rustling and the value of the booty hauled off by the thieves. Even in the 1970s a small pickup load of avocados could be worth several thousand dollars and once the product had left the farm, it was hard for a farmer or a sheriff to say exactly where the illicit goods had come from. As the price of avocados increases, so does the rustling problem. Owing to the limited resources of county sheriffs in the Southern California counties where production is concentrated, the California Avocado Commission has hired and deployed six full-time avocado cops to deter and investigate avocado theft.

Avocado rustling is problematic in all the places where avocados are grown because of the high value of the crop. It is particularly prevalent in New Zealand because their strict bio-security measures forbid the importation of avocados grown in other places. This means all demand for avocado in the country has to be met by New Zealand growers. As a result, New Zealand has some of the most expensive avocados in the world, sometimes selling for two to three times the average price of an avocado in the U.S. or Europe. The crop from a single tree can be worth thousands of New Zealand dollars, so even home growers are beginning to outfit their trees with security systems to deter thieves.

If the goal of the avocado marketers was to have an avocado on every table, the way American presidential candidate Herbert Hoover promised a chicken in every pot, then they are well on their way to accomplishing their goal. In a century they have taken the green fruit from near anonymity to near ubiquity. The Canadian journalist David Sax said, in *The Tastemakers* (2014), 'The avocado has gone from being this rare thing to a staple. I mean, I'm walking by my shitty

Honey bee pollinating an avocado flower, New Zealand.

Metro, and they have it, and the cheap Chinese grocery store has it. It's not cheap, but it isn't a luxury. It's not rare, like chia seeds. It's widely cultivated, it's familiar.' The avocado has gone from being virtually unknown to being one of the most important tropical or subtropical fruit crops in only a hundred years. The only other tropical or subtropical plants to gain this level of importance in the marketplace are the pineapple and the banana.

Avocado Nutrition: The Fattiest Fruit

Avocados are unusual fruits in that they contain virtually no sugar or starch. Also unusual for a fruit, they contain up to 30 per cent fat, the same level as in a sirloin steak (though the fat of the avocado is mostly the good kind, monounsaturated and polyunsaturated). In addition, avocados have the highest protein levels of any fruit, a boon for marketers in today's protein-mad world. When you factor in the high level of certain vitamins and minerals, avocados are probably the most nutrient-dense of all fruits. This high nutrient density was probably an evolutionary strategy on the part of the avocado to make sure it was chosen by the disperser megafauna. Today, many consumers think of the avocado as a 'unicorn' food, a foodstuff that tastes indulgent, but without negative health consequences. It is a food that consumers in both the health food store and the local McDonald's can agree on.

Avocados are high in monounsaturated fats and low in saturated fats, much like olive oil. Much of the energy density of the avocado comes from these fats. This high fat content nearly derailed the avocado on its way to becoming the aristocrat of salad fruits. In the 1970s avocados were a key ingredient in the much-admired California lifestyle and were

Trendy meets traditional in this visual mash-up of bacon and eggs with avocado on toast.

popular with both status seekers and natural/health food consumers. But the 1980s brought tough times for the avocado. This was the fat-free decade. Distinctions between good fats (monounsaturated) and bad fats (saturated) were not made. The McGovern Report of 1977 addressed the epidemic of heart disease in the United States and made dietary fat the primary villain. As a result, a flood of low-fat and fat-free products entered the marketplace (never mind that fat was replaced with some kind of sugar, often high-fructose corn syrup). Avocados were placed in the same class of foods as bacon, eggs and butter. Heart patients were given lists of food to avoid that put the avocado in the same category as well-marbled beef. The wholesale price of avocados dropped as low as ten cents a pound at their lowest point. There was such a glut of avocados on the market that processors scrambled for alternative uses. At one point there was a proposal to make an avocado-based dog food, notwithstanding the fact

Avocado smoothie.

that a number of substances in them can cause digestive misery for dogs. Only America's growing love of guacamole kept the orchards from being torn out and replaced with other crops. Avocado marketers from California fought back in the 1980s with a famous ad featuring sex symbol Angie Dickinson in a skin-tight white leotard eating an avocado and asking, 'Would this body lie to you?'

Since then, avocados have benefited from research that shows that certain fats, the monounsaturated ones in avocados among them, actually have health benefits. One benefit of the fat in avocados is the fact that it aids in creating satiety, a feeling of fullness that signals to the body that it has enough food and it is okay to stop eating. Still, calories are calories to many consumers. While popular varieties like the Hass have a relatively high fat content, there are various cultivars from the West Indian races that have significantly fewer calories from fat, and there is a movement afoot to market these as reduced-energy alternatives to Mexican and Guatemalan cultivars. One company, Brooks Tropicals LLC, is selling what used to be called the Florida avocado or the Hardee as the Slimcado®. This is an older variety grown in Florida that has about half the fat and about one-third fewer calories than the Hass. It has about the same protein level but is lower in most other nutrients. Reviews of the fruit on the Internet and in the print media have not always been kind to the Slimcado, but it does have a following. People who have eaten it report that it has a watery mouthfeel, where the Hass is creamy and unctuous, and has fruity undertones of mango instead of the familiar nutty flavour of the Hass. Due to their watery nature and fruit flavours, greenskin avocados are useful when making avocado drinks like smoothies.

Avocados are a good source of vitamins C and E, both valuable as antioxidants, as well as vitamins K and B-6. They are also good sources of the minerals copper and phosphorus. Avocados have twice as much potassium as bananas. The bioavailability of the lutein found in avocados is higher than almost any other fruit or vegetable. Avocados may reduce the pain associated with inflammation and are recommended by the Arthritis Foundation for people with osteoarthritis. The pigments in avocados are rich in the phytochemicals that provide many micro-nutrients.

Avocado Oil

As we have seen, avocados are a fatty fruit. The oil content of the richest avocados, such as the Hass and the Fuerte, can cross the 20 per cent threshold if they are allowed to mature properly. Most avocados are grown to sell as fresh whole fruit in the market. Fruit that is mostly uniform and usable, but considered unmarketable because of blemishes and such, is graded number two and is usually sent for processing into prepared guacamole and other avocado pulp products. This still leaves a good deal of fruit that is suitable for neither use and is available for other purposes. Today, that primarily means avocado oil production.

The highest-grade avocado oil goes into culinary products, and the rest is used in various cosmetic preparations. It can be used as seasoning oil, such as when we toss pasta with extra-virgin olive oil for the flavour it imparts, but it can also be used in frying. While it's expensive, avocado oil is well suited for frying as it has a high smoke point, 270°C (515°F), which is higher than many other oils used for this purpose. It is relatively stable at high heats due to its low levels of acid, and it resists breakdown owing to temperature better than many frying oils.

Avocado oil has also attracted a lot of attention owing to its perceived health properties. While often compared to extra-virgin olive oil, it is even lower in saturated fats, and its monounsaturated fatty acid level is higher. Avocado oil is also more neutral in flavour than extra-virgin olive oil, and even more so when the oil is heated. It has excellent keeping qualities. In an experiment in California, samples were kept at refrigerator temperature for ten years and showed only very slight evidence of rancidity.

Whereas most of the plant oils we use for culinary purposes come from the seed or nut of the plant (think corn, soybean, rapeseed (canola) and grapeseed oil), some come from the flesh of the fruit, as is the case with olive oil and coconut oil. There are several ways to extract the oil from the flesh of the avocado, and the method chosen depends on the level of technology the presser has access to and the end use of the oil.

The oldest method of extracting avocado oil is a boil and skim method. The pulp is crushed, mixed with water and simmered over low heat. The mixture is then cooled and the supernatant oil skimmed off. The skimmed oil is usually reheated and strained, but the methodology does allow a small level of impurities to remain. The method is crude, but if a producer cannot afford or otherwise has no access

Avocado oil, an increasingly popular product, promoted for its health benefits.

to more modern technology, it is effective, and the oil can be used in a variety of ways.

This method has been largely superseded by a process using chemical solvents. There are two variants of this process. One involves drying the pulp to get rid of water, mixing it with chemical solvents that enhance maximum extraction, then pressing it to extract the oil. The other process involves centrifuging the pulp to extract the oil cells, then treating the oil cells with chemical solvents to separate the pure oil from other elements in the oil cells. Both methods leave the oil in a state that requires further refinement to make it usable. After the further refinement, the oil is chemically pure, with high levels of emollients and vitamin E. The rough handling and the exposure to chemical solvents leave it undesirable as a culinary oil, but it is highly sought after by the cosmetic industry. Humectants in avocado oil help maintain a feeling of moisture in human skin, making it feel youthful and plump. Facial masks containing avocado oil have become popular in the spa industry where they are marketed as rejuvenating.

The most recent innovation in avocado oil extraction is cold pressing. Avocados are skinned and stoned before the pulp is cold pressed like olive oil. In fact, the original machines used to develop the process were cold-press olive oil presses brought in as an experiment. Hass and Fuerte are the most commonly used avocados for cold press extraction, since they are the cultivars with the highest oil content. Hass is especially desirable for cold pressing because the resulting oil is a pale emerald green that brings about an immediate association with the whole fruit. The colour can be enhanced by including some avocado skin, which is very high in chlorophyll, with the pulp in the press. Oils made with skin in the press tend to be brilliant emerald green. Cold-pressed avocado oil made from Hass fruit is said to taste like avocados, with a soupçon of grassy and mushroom odours. Fuerte-based oil is said to have more of the mushroom aroma and a less pronounced avocado flavour. Growers in New Zealand, Australia and the United States are working to develop terminology that will guide consumers in selecting different grades of avocado oil. The working documents suggest the grades will be much like those of olive oil (and therefore easy for consumers to understand): extra-virgin, virgin, pure and blend. Once the oil has been extracted, the pulp that remains is sold to the animal feed industry, as it still retains much of the protein.

Avocado oil is starting to see some applications in medicine. Many parts of the tree, fruit and leaf have always been a part of the folk medicine repertoire of Mesoamerica. Avocados were used to treat small wounds, especially abrasions, where they were thought to speed healing. Today homeopathic practitioners recommend avocado oil for medical conditions that simulate abrasion, such as sunburn, eczema and psoriasis. In France extracts from avocado oil and soybean oil have been combined and put into the pharmacopeia as a prescription drug. Going under the acronym ASU (Avocado-Soybean Unsaponifiables), it is prescribed for knee and hip osteoarthritis. In some countries ASU is available over the counter, and is recommended for various conditions caused by internal inflammation. Medical studies are beginning to suggest that avocado oil consumption can increase hepatic function in the liver, but this research is in its early days. Avocatin B, a substance isolated from avocado oil, is currently being tested in clinical medical trials as possibly useful in the fight against acute myeloid leukemia (AML).

Other parts of the avocado may be a boon to good health as well. The pulp of avocados is rich in antioxidants, fibre, minerals, vitamins and phytonutrients. There is evidence that eating avocados may help to prevent metabolic syndrome, a condition where a patient displays three or more risk factors for heart disease or diabetes, such as high blood pressure, high triglyceride levels or a large waistline. Avocados can help reduce LDL cholesterol (the bad kind), increase HDL cholesterol (the good kind) and reduce belly fat. Researchers are also looking at substances found in avocado stones as a source of medical treatments. The stones contain behenyl alcohol, a long-chain fatty alcohol used in anti-viral medications, and dodecanoic acid (also known as lauric acid, due to its presence in plants in the laurel family), which is used in various antiviral medications and has been studied for potential use in medicines for issues related to atherosclerosis.

4
Eating Avocados and Other Uses

The most popular way to eat avocados is in the form of guaca-mole. As noted earlier, Americans eat millions of pounds of it on Super Bowl Sunday alone, and who knows how much more the rest of the year. Most of the avocados bought in grocery stores are used to make guacamole, and premade guacamole is a staple of both grocers and food-service companies.

The early Mesoamericans were undoubtedly the first eaters of guacamole. As we have seen they have been eating avocados for millennia, and the home of avocados is also the home of maize. Tortillas arose early on as the preferred way to eat maize in Mesoamerica. It isn't much of a stretch to think of them being consumed together, even before American football became a television staple in that country. In fact there is archaeological evidence that suggests they were being eaten together in pre-Columbian times. The name 'guacamole' derives from the Nahuatl word *ahuaco-mulli*. When Hernán Cortés arrived in Tenochtitlán, what is now Mexico City, he found the court of Montezuma eating a mash of avocado, tomato, wild onion and coriander that his scribes rendered as *ahuacamulli*.

Recipes for guacamole have been published in the American press since the earliest days of avocado promotion.

Arguably Mexico's most popular culinary export: guacamole.

In 1912 the *New York Times* published a recipe for 'Aguacate Salad' made with the relatively novel alligator pear.

> Cut three ripe avocado pears in halves, take out the stones, and scrape the pulp from the skin. Add three tomatoes, first removing the skin and hard pieces around the stem end, and half a green pepper pod, cut in fine shreds. Crush and pound the whole to a smooth mixture, then drain off the liquid. To the pulp, add a teaspoonful

or more of onion juice and a generous teaspoonful of lemon juice or vinegar. Mix thoroughly and serve at once.

The *New York Times* has published many recipes for guacamole since 1912. The recipe published in 1953 suggested potato chips as the ideal accompaniment. In 2013 the newspaper published the infamous green pea guacamole recipe that started a Twitterstorm of controversy that was even weighed in on by the sitting president of the United States, Barack Obama.

The Online Entomological Dictionary says that the term 'guacamole' first appeared in the American lexicon in 1920, but early spellings varied. The silent-screen heartthrob Ramon Novarro contributed his recipe for the dish to the *Photoplay Cookbook* in 1929, and he used the modern spelling of the word.

The 1931 cookbook *Fashions in Food in Beverly Hills* from the Beverly Hill's Woman's Club spelled it *Wakimoli* and used the term *calavo* to refer to the avocados.

The *calavos* are halved, the stones removed, and the meat scraped from the half shells. Thoroughly mash the meat and stir finely chopped onions into it. Beat in mayonnaise dressing until the mixture attains the consistency of thick paste. Season with salt, pepper, and paprika. This may be served in the half shells, on lettuce, or is delicious on toasted crackers.

Another 1931 cookbook, the influential *Joy of Cooking*, had two recipes for avocados, called 'avocado pears' in the book. One was for a composed 'Avocado Pear Salad' and the other for 'Avocado Pear, Orange, and Grapefruit Salad'. The recipes are similar in tone to those published as part of the campaigns

Avocado salad, Kraft Mayonnaise advertisement in the *Ladies' Home Journal* (June 1948).

selling the avocado as the 'Aristocrat of Salad Fruits' where they were paired with grapefruit, lobsters and crab.

The doyenne of Mexican cookery, Diana Kennedy, in her seminal text *Cuisines of Mexico*, should have the last word about guacamole. She wrote, 'Never, never use a blender for the avocado to turn it into one those smooth, homogenous messes.' She also knew that, as with all avocado dishes, freshness is the key to guacamole. She advises eating the guacamole directly after it is prepared. If you wait, 'Almost immediately the delicate green will darken and the fresh, wonderful flavor will be lost.'

Other Culinary Uses

In its original home of Central America, the avocado has many culinary uses beyond guacamole. Many indigenous people in Central America still eat the traditional breakfast of tortillas with salted avocado slices and coffee. Salsa verde, a soupy mixture of avocado, tomatillo, coriander (cilantro) and onions, is used as a condiment on many savoury dishes. Sliced or diced avocados are used as a cooling garnish for foods with hot chillies. Chicken broth soups are popular all over Central America and South America. Slices and dice of fresh avocado are often floated on the top of the soup to add flavour and texture.

Avocados are used as a filling in a wide array of dishes, such as tacos, enchiladas, flautas, panuchos, salbutes and tortas. Avocado halves are stuffed with picadillo, ceviche or

Lentil soup with avocado.

Avocado coffee shake.

roasted chicken and served as a main course. Throughout the region avocados are among the most common salad ingredients. The leaves are used as a rub for *barbacoa*, the original form of barbecue, and are sometimes thrown into the fire to add an anise note. Leaves are also sometimes thrown into a pot of cooking beans for the same flavour addition.

As the avocado moved around the world, many cultures adopted and adapted the fruit in ways that complemented their local cuisine. In Brazil avocados tend to be consumed with added sugar in a variety of sweet dishes. A popular breakfast item is diced avocado stirred into sweetened condensed milk to make a sort of chunky milkshake. In Indonesia coffee and avocado milkshakes are popular, as are chocolate and avocado milkshakes. Pureed avocado pulp is mixed with sweetened coffee and drunk for breakfast or as a pick-me-up later in the day. In 1982 Mrs Murniata Widjaja won an Indonesian iced drink competition with her concoction of avocado, jackfruit, coconut, sweetened condensed milk and ice. She named the drink Es Teler, which roughly translates as 'drunk ice'. Her family decided to capitalize on the fame this award brought her and started a small business in a kiosk outside a large shopping centre, called *Es Teler 77* (77 being an auspicious number in the ethnically Chinese communities in Indonesia). The drink became wildly popular and the Widjajas began to franchise the operation. There are now more than two hundred outlets in Indonesia, Malaysia and Singapore, as well as four in Australia.

Coffee ready to pour over avocado ice cubes.

Sweet avocado drinks are common in Africa as well. In Morocco a milk and avocado drink sweetened with sugar and flavoured with orange-flower water is extremely popular and available in virtually every coffee shop or *malhaba* (dairy bar). In Ethiopia one of the most popular beverages is a drink called Spris. It is avocado pulp mixed with milk and sweetened with the fruity soft drink Vimto.

Savoury dishes with avocado are popular in sub-Saharan Africa. In Ghana, tea sandwiches, made by spreading avocado onto crispy baguettes, are sold on nearly every corner. A similar sandwich is sold on the streets of Haiti. In Peru bread sticks are stuffed with cheese and avocado, then deep fried. For Guatemalans, a status breakfast is an avocado half topped with scrambled eggs and anchovy fillets. In Japan avocado halves are eaten sprinkled with soy sauce and horseradish or wasabi.

For better or worse, the avocado has become the symbol of the millennial lifestyle. In 2018 the number of avocado-related hashtags on Instagram had passed the 400,000 mark,

Drunk Ice, *Es Teler*, Indonesia.

Avocado drink, Ethiopia.

with no sign of slowing. There are currently around 1.2 million posts of avocado toast available for ogling on Instagram alone, not to mention countless more photos of other avocado creations. According to the online service zoosk.com, mentioning your affection for guacamole will make you 144 per cent more likely to get a message from someone interested in going on a date with you. In 2018 Virgin Trains UK had a weeklong promotion wherein 26–30-year-old travellers (millennials) could get 33 per cent off a Millennial Railcard if they presented an avocado when they bought it. Avocados have become the signature food of the millennial generation.

For a generation consumed by online social media, the avocado is the perfect food. It is nutritious and flavourful,

The trendiest brunch: avocado toast. Here patterned in delightful rosettes.

and looks adorable. A popular online buzz phrase is 'let's avocuddle' and 2016 saw the arrival of the avocado emoji. Avocados are easy to prepare, are a guilt-free indulgence and look good on one's Instagram page. As consumption scholar Nathan Greenslit says: 'we don't consume individual objects; we consume the social order they belong to . . . when we buy (a product) we consume assumptions about genders, households, families, and social status.' Avocado consumption expresses these aspirations and assumptions for a millennial generation.

According to the *New Statesman*, the food most synonymous with the aspirational lifestyles of the first two decades of the twenty-first century is avocado toast. The current boom for avocado toast was said to have been set off by chef Bill Grainger in Melbourne in 1993, but the combination of avocados and toasted bread is much older. The early Spanish settlers in Mexico called avocados *mantequilla del pobre*, which means butter of the poor, suggesting that it was used this way from at least the earliest days of Spanish conquest. Mentions of avocado on toast seasoned with a bit of salt and pepper begin showing up in English sources as early as the 1840s. The first mention in American newspapers was in 1885 in the *Daily Alta Cal.* The *Corvina Argus* of San Gabriel, California, directed its readers to mash avocado with a fork and spread it on hot toast in 1920. The *San Francisco Chronicle* printed its own recipe in 1927. Writing in the *New Yorker* about the culture of Southern California in 1937, S. J. Perelman writes of avocado sandwiches on wheat toast washed down with lime rickeys in a way that suggests their ubiquity on health food menus leaves them open to derision. In 1962 the *New York Times* commented that an 'unusual' way to serve avocado is to make a 'toasted sandwich' with it. Grainger started selling avocado toast at his eponymous café, Bill's, in Melbourne, because his lease allowed him to be open only from 7:30 a.m. until 4 p.m. and he could not sell alcoholic beverages. Without profitable evening sales and the liquor sales that often go along with them, Grainger had to find ways to boost his prices during the breakfast hours when ticket averages were at their lowest. Avocado toast appeared to be part of the solution.

In 2017 John Birdsall wrote in *Bon Appetit* magazine that avocado toast signifies 'everything good, bad, elitist, humble, annoying, and yes, delicious about eating in America right now'. It went on to say that restaurants are 'eager to make bank on a dish with the easiest of odds: a vegetal-tasting fruit of supermarket ubiquity, spread onto the world's most common comfort food'. Gwyneth Paltrow featured avocado toast in her cookbook *It's All Good*, calling the combination of avocado, Vegenaise and sea salt 'the holy trinity', and likened it to 'a favorite pair of jeans, so reliable and easy and just what you want'. Once she had Gooped it, it was everywhere. The *New Yorker*, in an article by Nathan Heller titled 'A Grand Unified Theory of Avocado Toast', published on 13 July 2017, explained the popularity of avocado toast thus:

> [it is] a fashion-friendly food: small, nourishing, refined, easy to share, customizable. It could be eaten in prim fashion, with a fork and knife. It could be consumed with the hands, without drippings or squirts. Carbohydrate-phobic diners could eat the avocado off the bread without looking demented. The toast stays simple enough to be calorie-countable, or to be ordered by special request in unknown lands. And, avocados being what they are, it's guaranteed fresh: an avocado mash laid to rest for an hour is visibly the worse for wear. In this respect, it is the ultimate cosmopolitan food, a dish for familiar pursuits in unfamiliar settings.

British *Vogue* added that avocado toast made people feel more connected to their food because they made it themselves.

In Australia, as in many other places, avocado toast has been the focus of many negative comments about the millennial lifestyle. Millennials were described as 'profligate' by the Melbourne real-estate baron Tim Gurner for spending too much money on avocado toast and fancy coffee. He pointedly commented, 'When I was trying to buy my first home, I wasn't buying smashed avocado for $19 and four coffees at $4 each.' In an article titled 'Evils of the Hipster Cafe', a columnist for *The Australian*, Bernard Salt, chimed in too, saying, 'I have seen young people order smashed avocado with feta on five-grain toasted bread at $22 a pop and more. Twenty-two dollars several times a week could go towards the deposit on a house.' One Melbourne café responded by offering a $10 avocado toast special called 'The Retirement Plan'. In another joking response to this criticism, another Melbourne café owner created a drink called the avolatte. This is a latte served in a scooped-out avocado shell. Intended as an ironic response to the negative comments, the irony was lost and restaurants around the world began serving avolattes.

Avocado toast is popular in the u.s. and uk as well. Café Gitane in New York City is said to have ignited the current avocado toast craze in the u.s. When you see an Instagram picture of avocado toast dotted with red pepper flakes, this is, in a sense, a homage to Café Gitane, who have served their avocado toast this way since at least 2006. Avocado toast was so ubiquitous in the u.s. by 2017 that a protester at the inauguration of President Trump carried a sign that read, 'Put avocado on racism so white people will pay attention.' According to an article in *Time* magazine in 2017, credit card processing company Square estimated that Americans spent nearly a million dollars a month on avocado toast, with the average price at $6.78 a slice. Unsurprisingly, the highest per capita consumption in the u.s. was in San Francisco, home of America's first toast restaurant, The Mill. More surprising was the third-place town, Nashville, far more famous for country music and spicy fried chicken than edgy culinary concepts like avocado toast. In 2015 the uk grocer Waitrose reported a 30 per cent increase in avocado sales after a segment on Nigella Lawson's cookery programme showed viewers how to make avocado toast. (Though not all Britons were impressed. The *Daily Mail* reported on a viewer who mockingly commented, 'She'll be teaching us how to make a cuppa next.')

While avocado dishes are popular with customers, their high price is a perpetual concern for food-service operators. A price spike in 2016 led to their removal from many menus, with the result called 'avo-geddon' by one caterer. Chipotle regularly threatens to take avocado off the menu when prices of the fruit get too high, though this hasn't actually happened yet. Some operators use avocados as they would a seasonal dish, putting them on the menu when they are cheap and abundant, removing them when they are expensive. The high price of avocados has some food-service operators jokingly using the term 'guacamoolah'. During the Great Australian Avocado Shortage of 2016, avocado theft became a problem for merchants in that country. Some stores posted signs saying 'No cash or avocados kept on premises overnight.'

As with any ultrafashionable food, there was an anti-avocado backlash at the height of its popularity. It was banned at the London cafes Wildflower and Firedog (the former asking people to take up swedes as their new fashionable vegetable) owing to the high social and environmental costs. The increasing use of the hashtag #overcado suggests that perhaps the avocado has jumped the shark among elite influencers.

Avocados are moving onto the cocktail menu as well. The Boston Avocado Cocktail uses avocado-flavoured vodka pureed with kale and lime to create a drink served in a coupe with a rim of breadcrumbs and cayenne. For colder weather, the Avocado Hot Toddy is made with tea brewed with whole avocado stones and tequila, then sweetened with agave syrup.

The Dutch alcoholic beverage called *advocaat* is a thick, egg-yolk-rich liqueur. The food writer Victoria Hansen claims it was invented in the Dutch colony of Surinam on the northern coast of South America and was originally made with avocados. The original concoction was supposedly a mash of avocado mixed with a lot of brandy and sugar. Legend has it that when the Dutch were thrown out of their sugar-processing colony of New Holland on the northeastern

Chocolate cake with avocado buttercream filling.

coast of Brazil in 1654, some of them moved on to Dutch colonies in Indonesia, taking avocado seedlings and the recipe with them. The story goes that avocado trees wouldn't grow in cold, damp Holland, so with thirst being the mother of invention, returnees craving the drink looked around for a fatty, creamy substitute for the avocado and turned to egg yolks. The Dutch word for lawyer is the same as for the liqueur. Supposedly the thick nature of the liqueur was good for the scratchy throat of a lawyer who talked all day, so it was originally named *advocaatenborrel* or lawyer's drink, which then was shortened to *advocaat*.

Other Parts, Other Uses

While the flesh is the most commercially valuable part of the avocado, other parts can be used as well. When avocado stones are crushed, they yield a liquid that looks like almond milk. After exposure to oxygen, the liquid turns a dark reddish-brown. This liquid was used as ink by the indigenous people of Mesoamerica and was adopted by the Spanish conquerors of Central and South America to write their legal documents and manuscripts. It is quite stable, and early documents that

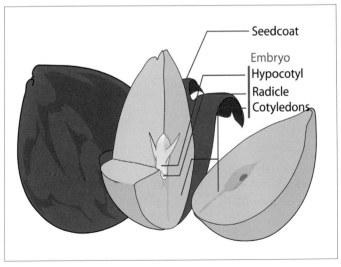

Avocado seed diagram showing the embryo at the fruit's interior.

Maluma avocado orchard, South Africa.

used it are still legible today. At one time, avocado ink was used to mark clothing owing to its indelible nature.

Mesoamericans also used a diluted form of the liquid as an early form of rouge. Ground avocado seed and skin are used as fabric dyes. Fabric coloured with avocado and other vegetable dyes was gently simmered with strips of avocado bark to set the dyes. The indigenous peoples of Mesoamerica sometimes mixed the flesh of avocados into the loose clay mixture they used for adobe.

The wood of avocado trees has little value beyond firewood. It is beautiful and is used to some extent in decorative woodcraft, but it is brittle, attracts termites and can discolour from infections caused by fungi present in the wood. Visually it is said to resemble the wood of the eucalyptus tree.

Various parts of the avocado are used in homeopathic remedies. Folk medicines often have remedies based in the ancient humoral system of causes and cures. Some parts, like the leaf of the tree, are considered dry and warm and are prescribed when a person's problems are 'cold and wet'. Conversely, the flesh is considered cool and damp and is prescribed when the patient's symptoms indicate a cause that is 'hot and dry'.

In Mexico avocado skin is used in compresses to suppress coughs and to speed the healing of bruises. Research has shown minor antibiotic-style compounds in the skin, but other chemicals in the skin may be deleterious to overall health. The seed is roasted, ground and consumed as a treatment for diarrhoea and dysentery. Ground seeds have astringent qualities and are used where these properties are needed. Homeopathic practitioners make a poultice from the pulp that is spread on the scalp to promote hair growth and the ground stone is said to fight dandruff. In Nigeria the stone is powdered and used as a treatment for hypertension. Recent medical research suggests medical efficacy in this practice, though the research should be regarded as preliminary. The ground seed is used in some places as a larvicide and an antifungal remedy.

In some practices of homeopathic medicine leaves from the tree are chewed to treat pyorrhoea. Leaf tea is drunk to control diarrhoea, soothe sore throats and regulate menstrual flow. New leaf shoots are boiled with crushed avocado stone to make an abortifacient. Using leaves in homeopathic cures should be approached with caution. Avocado leaves contain persin, a fungicidal toxin that can disrupt cellular DNA function as well as cause colic and various gastrointestinal diseases.

Appendix:
Types of Avocado

Hass While the Hass dominates the retail market for avocados, there are literally hundreds of varieties grown by small commercial producers and smallholders growing for personal consumption. Commercial producers of avocados group them into one major cultivar, the Hass. Every other type of avocado is classed as a minor cultivar, such is its ubiquity. Consumers are accustomed to avocados being available year-round, but like most food crops, avocados are seasonal. The season for Hass avocados grown in the USA is roughly April to September. Hass avocados are grown at many different elevations in Michoacán, Mexico, which makes them available nearly year-round, but avocados grown there are at their best from August to April. These overlapping seasons, and advances in storage technology, made the Hass the first avocado to be available year-round in the markets of the Americas. That the growing market for Hass avocados in Europe is fed from both sides of the equator means avocados are available to consumers year-round in these markets as well.

Fuerte While the Hass is the primary cultivar in widespread commerce, that place was once held by the Fuerte variety. The name means 'strong', a moniker it earned after being virtually the only cultivar to survive the famous 'Freeze of '13' in Southern California. The Fuerte is about the size of a Hass with a leathery skin and an oily flesh with a yellow cast. It mostly stays green when ripe, so ripeness is ascertained by pressing on the skin to assess the softness of the flesh underneath. This unctuous cultivar ripens throughout the winter months and has a flavour reminiscent of hazelnuts. Among the avocado cognoscenti, the Fuerte is considered to have the best taste of all avocados. Fuertes remain at peak ripeness longer than other popular varieties, which almost all go from ripe to rotten in very short order. Most of the 'cocktail avocados' on the market are Fuertes that have somehow escaped sexual development.

Shepard The Shepard is similar to the Fuerte. While it originated and is grown in the Northern Hemisphere, it has found its greatest acceptance in Australia. Though it is often compared to the Fuente or Hass for flavour, the texture is sometimes described as gluey, which has probably limited its popularity. It has one of the slowest rates of oxidation of any avocados, which means it browns very slowly when cut. Although it is a good choice for avocado toast, perhaps explaining its popularity in Australia, it is not recommended for guacamole.

Reed Produce buyer for Whole Foods James Parker says the Reed may be the avocado with the most potential to challenge the dominance of the Hass. The Reed is a large avocado, about the size of an American softball or English lawn bowling ball, and often weighs nearly 450 grams (1 lb). It has a comparatively large seed, but owing to the overall size of the fruit, it produces more edible flesh than the Hass. The flesh is yellowish-green with a buttery, nutty flavour much like that of the Hass. The growing season of the Reed is shorter than the Hass, but it produces more pounds per acre than the Hass does with less water per acre, which could give it an advantage in the main growing areas in California, where land and water become more expensive by the year. This ability to thrive with less water has made the Reed popular with growers in Australia, where irrigation water is at a premium. It is a green-skin avocado, which means ripeness must be tested by pressing on the skin and assessing softness.

GEM GEM avocados are another avocado with the potential to dethrone the Hass. Named for the breeder who developed it at the University of California, Gray E. Martin, the GEM is a grand-daughter of the Hass avocado by way of the Gwen. It has many of the flavour and textural attributes of the Hass but yields more fruit per tree and the tree is more compact, meaning harvest is less costly. It ripens after most of the Hass crop has gone to market, so it could be an excellent companion product, allowing American avocados to be in stores year-round. It can also hang on the tree for longer periods without compromising fruit quality, giving growers more time to harvest it. Growers also appreciate the fact that it is less prone to a biennial fruiting pattern than the Hass. The GEM is a green-skin variety, but when ripe it has lovely gold flecks, giving it visual appeal for retail consumers as well as visual ripeness clues. It often outscores the Hass in blind taste panels. The GEM also has the slowest oxidation rate of any avocado in widespread commerce, meaning that it doesn't turn brown as fast once cut. This could make it very popular with food-service operators as well as retail consumers. The GEM has gained acceptance with European consumers and is a featured variety at Tesco stores in the UK.

Lamb Hass The Lamb Hass is a cross-bred avocado with a considerable amount of the original Hass in its genetic makeup. It is larger than a regular Hass, often weighing in over 450 grams (1 lb). It has a flavour that rates nearly as highly as the original Hass and turns black as it ripens, which makes it easy to market to consumers trained to look for colour as an indicator of ripeness. It is harvested later than the original Hass, so it can be a good companion avocado in the marketplace. Its large size may not be a plus with marketers, but plantings are on the increase in California growing regions.

Pinkerton The Pinkerton is a limited season California avocado with a small seed and scores highly in flavour and texture tests. Growers like the fact that wood is less brittle than the Hass, making the tree sturdier and less susceptible to wind damage. Many avocado aficionados feel the flavour of the Pinkerton is even richer than the Hass, while maintaining its desirable texture. The Pinkerton gets dark blotches on the skin when ripe, giving consumers visual clues to ripeness. Given the short growing season and limited plantings, the Pinkerton may only ever be a niche avocado, but one worth seeking out.

Bacon The Bacon avocado gets its name from the farmer who first developed it, James Bacon (not, unfortunately, because it tastes like bacon – that would truly make it a unicorn food). The Bacon is a Guatemalan-race avocado, which means that it is lower in fat and has a higher water content than Mexican-race varieties like the Hass. Bacon avocados are lightly sweet, which, combined with the higher water content, make them the ideal avocado for smoothies. The Bacon is a green skin cultivar, which means ripeness is assessed by pressing on the skin. Like the Zutano, which is similar in flavour and texture, the Bacon is primarily grown to serve as a B-type pollinator for the Hass and much of the fruit is sent to processors, with only a small amount available as whole fruit in the retail market.

Sharwil The Sharwil is a cross of Mexican and Guatemalan-race avocados created in Australia, where the variety remains popular. Sharwils are also common in Hawaii, where they are the main cultivar in commercial production (as well as being grown extensively in yards and home gardens). The Sharwil has one of the smallest stones of the commercially produced avocados. Combined with the fact that they can grow quite large (the world record avocado – nearly 2.5 kilograms (5 ½ lb) – was a Hawaiian Sharwil), this means that the fruit gives a significant amount of edible flesh for the size of the fruit. Australian Sharwils tend to be smaller than the Kona sub-cultivar grown in Hawaii. The fruit is oily like a Hass, giving it a desirable mouthfeel and flavour. Sharwils are classified as a green-skin avocado, but some turn a very dark green as they ripen, mimicking the Hass. Overall, the Sharwil is considered a superior avocado. The USDA restricted Kona Sharwil importation into the continental United States for a number of years owing to concerns about pest transfer, but this ban has been rescinded to the extent that Sharwils are now allowed into cold weather states and are seen on the east coast of the u.s.

Choquette The Choquette is sometimes called the Florida avocado in recognition of it being the most widely grown avocado there. It is a Mexican-Guatemalan hybrid that has one of the largest fruits in widespread commerce. The flavour and texture are desirable and it is highly resistant to the numerous pests of Florida, which has led to its ubiquity in the state. Choquettes have one of the lowest fat contents of any avocado and are frequently called 'diet avocados' by marketers. Their low fat content is largely due to the high amount of water in the fruit, a trait common to most varieties grown in Florida. Although the water content is higher than other popular cultivars, the choquette retains its shape nicely when cut and mashes well for guacamole. The choquette is popular on the east coast of the United States, where it had become well established commercially before the Hass marketing blitz.

Mexicola Grande The Mexicola Grande is a version of the classic Mexicola avocado. These are the newest must-have variety for avocado geeks. Starting out bright yellow, then turning dark purple, the Mexicola Grande looks more like a baby aubergine than an avocado and has a paper-thin skin that is easily pierced with a fingernail. Like that of a cocktail avocado, the peel of the Mexicola Grande is edible, though not as palatable as the former. The flavour is described as very nutty and extremely rich. The leaves are edible and have a pronounced anise aroma. Unusually for avocados, the Mexicola Grande is an efficient self-pollinator and grows well in pots. It is perhaps the most cold and frost-tolerant avocado and will grow in areas at least one to two zones colder than other varieties.

For those interested in growing an avocado tree in a pot indoors that might actually produce fruit the Mexicola Grande is probably the best bet. Trees of this cultivar are available from a number of sources on the Internet. Shipping of agricultural products across jurisdictional borders is often restricted, so enquire before making an online purchase.

Recipes

The Internet has page after page of ways to use avocados, mostly in their raw state. This is with good reason. The longer avocados are subjected to cooking temperatures, the more bitter they become. Exposure to heat causes most food products to oxidize. In foods with a high enough sugar content, this causes caramelization or the Maillard reaction, which is mostly desirable. In avocados exposure to heat causes the fatty acids to oxidize and transform into oxylipids, which get stronger in flavour and more bitter the longer they are at oxidation-inducing temperatures. The tannins in avocados also express a bitter flavour when heated. If you want to have avocado in a cooked dish, it is better to add it just before serving, as is the case in the chicken-broth soups with avocado cubes that are popular in Mexico and Central America. If it is essential to cook the avocado, minimizing time at high temperatures will temper the bittering effect slightly.

The most popular use of the avocado is for making guacamole. This speciality originated in ancient Mexico and has been adopted by cultures around the world. The key to superior guacamole is simplicity. A perfectly ripe avocado, a few ingredients and minimal handling will result in a flavourful and toothsome dip. The variants are endless and a Google search will result in tens of millions of hits. A recipe for guacamole called 'avocado salad' was in the first Bulletin of the u.s. Department of Agriculture about avocados in 1905 and recipes have proliferated ever since.

Commonalities in most recipes include some member of the onion family, citrus juice (usually lime or lemon), some type of Mexican seasoning like cumin or coriander (cilantro), tomatoes, a bit of spicy capsicum such as jalapeño, and salt. Most recipes purporting to be authentic use chopped coriander, but the soapy flavour of the herb has as many detractors as enthusiasts. The following recipe is the author's favourite, but feel free to add or omit ingredients to make it your own. Purists will scream at the use of mayonnaise and soy sauce, but they add a lot to the texture, colour and flavour.

Miller's Guacamole

2 perfectly ripe avocados
juice of 2 small limes or 1 large lemon
1 small Roma tomato, cut into small dice
1 large shallot or ½ small red onion, minced
¼ teaspoon ground cumin
1 teaspoon Louisiana-style hot sauce or Tabasco sauce
½ teaspoon soy sauce
1 teaspoon mayonnaise
optional: ½–1 small jalapeño, minced, and a bit of chopped coriander (cilantro)

Peel the avocados and remove the stone. Cut into a fairly large dice and put into a mixing bowl.

Squeeze the limes or lemon through a strainer over the diced flesh. Gently stir in the juice until the cubes are well coated.

Fold in the tomato, onion (jalapeño and/or coriander if using), cumin, hot sauce, soy sauce and mayonnaise. Stir only as needed to incorporate. The avocado will break down quickly as it is stirred and the best guacamole is somewhat chunky, so stir as little as needed to just incorporate the ingredients. Taste and adjust seasoning with salt and black pepper as needed. Serve immediately with your preferred style of tortilla chips. (While many avocado cultivars can be used to make delicious guacamole, some greenskin varieties have a tendency to weep after cutting and mashing. This can be somewhat countered by using mayonnaise in the recipe, but guacamoles made with greenskin avocados will be moister than those made with the Hass.)

Pea Guacamole

During the Obama administration, one of the biggest Twitter-storms occurred when the president gave a thumbs down to green-pea-enhanced guacamole. The original, from Jean-Georges Vongerichten of Jean-Georges fame, included toasted sunflower seeds. The following recipe doesn't include those but might be good with fish and chips, because it is essentially good old English mushy peas with some avocado. While it may infuriate the guacamole purists, it is actually quite tasty.

225 g (8 oz) shelled green peas (garden peas), fresh or frozen
1 small clove garlic, minced
juice of 1 small lemon or lime
1 small Roma tomato, chopped
¼ teaspoon ground cumin
1 teaspoon Louisiana-style hot sauce or Tabasco sauce
1 or 2 avocados, peeled and cut into large dice
salt and ground black pepper to taste

Combine the peas with the garlic in a saucepan with a few table-spoons of water and cook at a low temperature until they are extremely soft. Don't allow to dry out and scorch, but try and have the pan nearly dry by the end of the cook time. Drain off any remaining liquid.

Add the lemon/lime juice and combine well. If you want the best texture, take the peas, garlic and lemon juice and puree them in a food processor, but this isn't necessary; you can just mash the peas with a fork or masher.

Stir in the remaining ingredients and then adjust the seasoning with salt and pepper to taste.

Avocado Margarita

A margarita is considered the best accompaniment to guacamole and tortilla chips. Of course, you could make that an avocado margarita.

75 ml (2.5 oz) good-quality white (blanco) tequila
30 ml (1 oz) honeydew melon liqueur
30 ml (1 oz) orange liqueur (Grand Marnier or Cointreau
are the best)
juice of one lime
30 ml (1 oz) honey or agave nectar
½ an avocado, peeled and stoned
70 g (½ cup) crushed ice

Combine all ingredients in a blender and puree until smooth. Serve in a salt-rimmed glass.

Avocado Toast

The ultimate millennial dish. Scorned and praised in equal measure, it may be the first dish of the millennial generation to secure a place in the longer-term culinary canon. A recipe is probably not really needed, but here are some guidelines.

Use whatever your favourite bread is, white or wholegrain. A bread with a bit of sugar in the recipe will brown nicely in the toaster and give a desirable hint of sweetness to the dish.

Spoon out the avocado flesh and place on the toast. Use a fork to mash it down and spread it around. As with guacamole, a bit of chunkiness is desirable. Season with salt and pepper. Beyond this, just about any add-on is fine. The classic is red pepper flakes, but anything from anchovy to za'atar is acceptable.

Avocado and Grapefruit Salad

Pairing avocados and grapefruit has been popular from the earliest days of avocado marketing. Both were novel foods in the years before the First World War and recipes using them were considered upscale. The California Avocado Commission printed its first recipe for the salad in the 1920s. The venerable *Joy of Cooking* had two variants on this classic in its very first edition in 1931. Alice Waters reprised it in the *New York Times* in 2010. In between, countless books, magazines and newspapers offered up a take on it. This classic combination appears never to go out of fashion.

> 1 ruby red grapefruit, peeled and sectioned
> 1 white grapefruit, peeled and sectioned
> 1 or 2 avocados, peeled and cut into wedges
> vinaigrette dressing to taste

Arrange the grapefruit and avocado alternately in a sunburst pattern. Dress with vinaigrette.

This arrangement can be served atop salad greens for a larger salad.

(Feel free to use all of one kind of grapefruit or the other. The California lifestyle magazine *Sunset* has published variants of this salad with additions of everything from smoked almonds to shrimp. This recipe can be dressed up or dressed down as required. To make the classic 1950s American version, use Kraft Catalina Dressing instead of vinaigrette.)

Crab Louis Salad

Another California original is Shrimp or Crab Louis. The first recipe for it was published in San Francisco in 1914 and called for asparagus instead of avocado. But avocado quickly became the green vegetable of choice for this dish and the combination of avocado and shellfish has become firmly rooted as most people's idea of the dish. All recipes claiming authenticity use iceberg lettuce as the base, but romaine is an excellent substitute. In America, the name of the salad is pronounced Looey, as in King Louis or Louis Davenport, a purported originator of the dish.

iceberg lettuce, washed and shredded
1 English cucumber, thinly sliced
2 medium fresh tomatoes, cut into wedges
2 large hard-boiled eggs, sliced
100 g tin (3.8 oz can) black olive slices
2 avocados, slices or large dice
450 g (1 lb) cleaned Dungeness crab or cooked, peeled prawns (shrimp) if preferred
prepared Louis dressing to taste (recipe follows)

Line 4 plates with shredded iceberg lettuce. Top with the sliced cucumber, then wedges of fresh, ripe tomato. Arrange slices of egg and olives over the lettuce and vegetables. Top with diced or sliced avocado, then distribute the crab or prawns over the vegetables. Top with Louis dressing and serve immediately.

Louis dressing:
230 g (1 cup) mayonnaise
115 g (½ cup) tomato ketchup
1 tablespoon horseradish sauce
1 teaspoon Worcestershire sauce
1 teaspoon lemon juice
dash of ground cayenne pepper
⅛ teaspoon garlic powder
25 g (¼ cup) minced spring (green) onion

Combine the mayonnaise, ketchup, horseradish sauce, Worcester-shire sauce, lemon juice, cayenne and garlic powder. Blend well. Fold in the onion. Chill and serve over the salad.

In a dire emergency one could use prepared Thousand Island dressing in place of Louis dressing, but it is inferior.

Shrimp Louis Appetizer

For true decadence, the Shrimp Louis appetizer reigns supreme.

2 avocados, peeled, split into halves and stoned
450 g (1 lb) cooked shrimp (a smaller shrimp is nice here)
Louis dressing
lemon wedges for garnish

Place the avocado halves on lettuce-leaf-lined plates. Combine the cooked shrimp with enough Louis dressing to bind it and make it creamy. Top each of the 4 avocado halves with a quarter of the shrimp mixture. Serve with the lemon wedges.

Avocado Poke Bowl

Avocado and seafood is a match made in heaven. Avocados pair as wonderfully with fin fish as they do with shellfish. Poke bowl, a Hawaiian dish that has taken the world by storm, is completed by the addition of avocado.

175 g (1 cup) cooked sushi rice
100 g (3.5 oz) prepared wakame salad
115 g (4 oz) sushi-grade tuna or salmon, or a combination
of the two
1 avocado, cut into thick slices or large dice
spicy mayonnaise or soy sauce
toasted white sesame seeds
toasted sesame oil

Place the cooked sushi rice in the bottom of a deep bowl. Top with the prepared wakame salad.

Gently mix the fish and the avocado and place over the wakame salad. Dress with as much spicy mayonnaise or soy sauce as desired. Garnish with sesame seeds and sesame oil.

Avocado Crema

Avocado Crema is a multi-purpose delight. This Mexican style crema is based on the very thin avocado sauces you get at street taco stands all over the western United States and in Mexico. You can use it on just about any salad or roasted meat. Of course it pairs extremely well with all of the Tex-Mex and Southern California-style Mexican classics like enchiladas, burritos, tacos and fajitas. This is an excellent recipe for using up ripe avocados or avocado flesh that has been frozen. It will keep for about a week in the refrigerator (but it usually doesn't last that long!).

15 g (½ oz) flat leaf parsley or coriander (cilantro),
washed and drained
2 tablespoons white vinegar
juice of 1 lime
120 ml (½ cup) water
2 spring (green) onions, coarsely chopped
¼ teaspoon red pepper flakes
½ teaspoon salt
½ teaspoon sugar
300 g (1 cup) Greek yoghurt
1 ripe avocado, peeled and stoned

Combine the parsley or coriander, vinegar, lime juice, water, spring onion, red pepper flakes, salt and sugar in a blender. Blend until the herbs and onion are pulverized into the liquid. Add the yoghurt and the avocado. Puree until smooth.

(Note: This is meant to be fairly thin, not thick like guacamole. Adjust with water as needed to give a thin salad-dressing consistency.)

Avocado and Coffee Breakfast Shake

Avocado and coffee is a popular combination in Brazil, Indonesia and the Philippines. An avocado-coffee shake is a common breakfast item in these countries.

1 ripe avocado, peeled and stoned
120 ml (4 oz) skimmed milk
225 g (8 oz) sweetened condensed milk
1–2 teaspoons instant espresso powder or 1 to 2 shots
of prepared espresso coffee
150 g (1 cup) crushed ice
optional: 1 teaspoon vanilla extract
optional: 90 ml (¼ cup) Autocrat-brand or Coffee Time-brand
coffee syrup

Place all ingredients in a blender and blend until smooth.

Further Reading

The Era of the Megaherbivore

Megaherbivores, plant-eating animals weighing more than 1,000 kilograms (2,200 lb), are now rare. Most of these giants are now found in sub-Saharan Africa and southern Asia. But in the Pleistocene, they were found on virtually every continent and took many forms. They were regulators of grassland and woodland ecosystems and important dispersers of fleshy fruits with large seeds. For many years it was thought that early humans hunted most of the megaherbivores to extinction, but today it is felt that they were already on their way out owing to climatic changes and that humans merely cleaned out the remnant populations of the few that survived into the modern era.

There are a number of plants whose primary dispersal mechanism was ingestion of and defecation by these huge plant-eating animals. Megaherbivores were indispensable in spreading the avocado from its early, limited range in the central Mexican highlands, though they were later spread even further by humans. The ecologists Dan Janzen and Paul Martin proposed that there were plants that should have gone extinct due to the lack of megaherbivore dispersers but did not. They called these plants 'ghosts' in their seminal paper, 'Neotropical Anachronisms: The Fruits the Gomphotheres Ate', *Science*, 215 (1982), pp. 19–27.

One of the most interesting explorations of this plant–animal relationship is *The Ghosts of Evolution: Nonsensical Fruits, Missing*

Partners, and Other Ecological Anachronisms (New York, 2000) by Connie Barlow. Barlow calls fruits like the avocado 'ghosts of evolution' because they survive long after their primary pre-human dispersers became extinct. This topic is also explored by Gary Nabhan in his book *Enduring Seeds* (San Francisco, CA, 1989).

The Botany of Avocados

While avocados had been noted from the earliest days of European contact with the New World, serious botanical scholarship is mostly a product of the twentieth and twenty-first centuries. The most comprehensive title on the topic is undoubtedly *The Avocado: Botany, Production and Uses* (Wallingford, 2013), an edited volume inspired by the quadrennial meetings of the World Avocado Congress. They have collected much valuable scholarship on avocado science, agriculture and technology.

Avocado Horticulture

For those interested in more detailed technical information about avocado cultivars and technical issues such as selection, propagation and orchard management, the California Avocado Commission and the University of California Extension Service offer an excellent two-book series that is available free online: Mary Arpaia et al., *Avocado Production in California: A Cultural Handbook for Growers*, 2nd edn (San Diego, CA, 2013), vol. I: *Background Information*, and vol. II: *Cultural Care*.

The California Avocado Commission also self-publishes a concise guide to best practices in avocado growing, *Growing for Quality: A Good Agricultural Practices Manual for California Avocado Growers, Version 1.0* (Irvine, CA, n.d.), available online at www.calavo. com/store/pdfs/gap.pdf. It contains detailed colour photographs of various pests and diseases as well as tips for hygiene and safety in the orchard.

Avocados in the Early Modern Period

Avocados were well known to the early Spanish and English explorers and exploiters in Mesoamerica and the Caribbean in the early modern period but were little more than a curiosity for most westerners until the second half of the nineteenth century, when agriculturists in Southern California and Florida began to suspect they had commercial potential. Guy Collins, a researcher for the United States Department of Agriculture, travelled widely in Mesoamerica researching avocados in the earliest years of the twentieth century and produced the first extensive manuscript on the topic, which was published as USDA Plant Industry Bulletin Number 77 in 1905. This bulletin set the tone and parameters for almost all future research on the topic of avocados.

The establishment of the California Ahuacate Organization in 1915 led to extensive research around avocado selection, propagation, orcharding and marketing. The organization later changed its name to the California Avocado Association and issues yearbooks annually. These yearbooks contain a trove of information about the evolution of the industry and its efforts to market the fruit to the public. Wilson Popenoe, an early advocate for avocados, wrote extensively for the yearbook about the history of the fruit, especially the early days of the industry in California. Many of these annual yearbooks are available online through avocadosource.com, a website maintained by the Hofshi Foundation for the dissemination of information about avocados, especially growing and orcharding.

The Avocado in Popular Culture

The avocado has become an object of fascination, adoration and (lately) ridicule in popular culture and social media. Pretty much any popular magazine, website or blog reporting on food has articles and posts featuring recipes and nutritional information (and sometimes misinformation) about avocados. A Google search of the term 'avocado' will turn up literally millions of hits.

The popularity of the fruit on social media platforms make it one of the most photographed foods. Some of the more serious writing about avocados in modern culture has been published in magazines and newspapers such as *The Atlantic*, the *New Yorker*, the *New York Times* and *The Guardian*.

As one might imagine, for a food that has conquered the popular imagination in the way that avocados have, there are a number of cookbooks on the topic including some dedicated to the singular topic of avocado toast. A selection of useful cookbooks include:

Dalkin, Gaby, *Absolutely Avocados* (New York, 2013)
An illustrated cookbook with an appetizing array of avocado dishes.

Dike, Colette, *The Ultimate Avocado Cookbook: 50 Modern, Stylish, and Delicious Recipes to Feed Your Avocado Addiction* (New York, 2019)
As the title indicates, stylish recipes with *au courant* ingredients.

Ferroni, Lara, *An Avocado a Day* (Seattle, WA, 2017)
This cookbook offers a wide range of recipes from breakfast to dessert with pictures of each recipe.

Other interesting short titles include:

Super Food: Avocado (London, 2017)
This book contains general titbits about avocados, recipes and a number of formulae for products such as avocado facial masks, shampoo and even fabric dye.

Langley, Andrew, *The Little Book of Avocado Tips* (Bath, 2018)
Another light reading generalist text with tips on avocado selection and care, recipes and so on.

Websites and Associations

The California Avocado Commission website offers information about varieties, ripening tips and recipes. It is the official site of the avocado marketer's association.
www.californiaavocado.com

Avocados from Mexico is the website of the Mexican Avocado Marketers. Lots of links to lore, tips and recipes.
https://avocadosfrommexico.com

The California Avocado Commission is the organization that represents avocado growers in California. The website links to resources about avocado husbandry.
www.californiaavocadosociety.org

Calavo is the the largest marketing cooperative for avocados. The website offers links to recipes and avocado tips and also some insights into the business of selling avocados.
www.calavo.com/store/home.php

Avocadosource is a clearing house for many types of agricultural information on avocados. It is also the archive for the California Avocado Association yearbooks, an invaluable research tool on the topic.
www.avocadosource.com

The Hass Avocado Board focuses solely on the one variety.
It is narrow, but deep. It offers production and consumption
data as well as a regular newsletter.
www.hassavocadoboard.com

Acknowledgements

Thanks to Micheal Leaman of Reaktion Books and Andrew Smith, the editor of the Edible series, for giving me the opportunity to write this book. The idea for the book was hatched over dinner with the two of them at the Oxford Symposium on Food and Cookery and I am so grateful it was allowed to come to fruition.

A special thanks to my department head, Dr Michael Pagliassotti. My research is somewhat out of step with what other people in my department do. He is incredibly supportive of my marching to the beat of a different drummer and I am grateful to him for that.

Photo Acknowledgements

The author and the publishers wish to express their thanks to the below sources of illustrative material and/or permission to reproduce it.

Alamy: pp. 45 (Kirn Vintage Stock), 82 (Brett Gundlock); author's Collection: pp. 17, 78, 85; California Avocado Association: pp. 35 (Zachary Benedict), 51, 52, 56, 57; CoffeePassion: p. 109; Dontworry: p. 33; Bernard Dupont: p. 10; Edrean: pp. 72, 119; Mark Hofstetter: p. 53; Hungda: p. 88; iStockphoto: p. 6 (FotografiaBasica); JackintheBox: p. 73; Jennifer: p. 107; Gunawan Kartapranata: p. 111; LACMA (Los Angeles County Museum of Art): p. 28 (Purchased with funds provided by the Bernard and Edith Lewin Collection of Mexican Art Deaccession Fund M.2014.89.2); LadyofHats: p. 118; Andrew Mandemaker: p. 93; The Metropolitan Museum of Art, New York: p. 77 (The Jefferson R. Burdick Collection. Gift of Jefferson R. Burdick. Accession Number: 63.350.201.12.3); naretmx: p. 11; Rick J. Pelleg: p. 55; PikWizard: p. 46; Pixabay: p. 68 (ceguito); Pixnio (USAID): p. 71; Wilson Popenoe: p. 13; Raw Pixel: p. 89 (Edgar Castrejon); Pavel Riha: p. 15; Rafael Saldaña: p. 62; The San Diego Museum of Art: p. 29 (Museum Purchase with funds provided by Dean and Mrs Michael H. Dessent and the Latin American Arts Committee. Accession Number: 2001.17); Shutterstock: p. 108 (Moch Fathor Rozi); Forest and Kim Starr: p. 49; Bukulu Steven: p. 66; Storyblocks.com: pp. 96 (pantermedia), 99,

104 (allisomari); Unsplash: pp. 95 (Stoica Ionela), 112 (Brenda Godinez); USAID (U.S. Agency for International Development): p. 69; U.S. Department of Agriculture Pomological Watercolor Collection, Rare and Special Collections, National Agricultural Library, Beltsville, MD: pp. 25, 36, 37, 40; U.S. Patent Office: p. 41; Vegan Feast Catering: p. 117 (Janet Hudson).

Index

italic numbers refer to illustrations; **bold** to recipes